Food on a Budget
Meals for Beginners

Notes on currencies and recipes:
Please note that where monetary equivalents are given they have either been presumed to be
like-for-like (i.e. £1 = US$1) or the exchange rate of 1.375 dollars to the pound has been applied where appropriate.
Please note that the measurements provided in this book are presented as metric/imperial/US-cups, using practical equivalents;
certain foods and cooking items that are termed differently in the UK and in North America are presented as
'UK term'/'US term'; and eggs are medium (UK)/large (US), and large (UK)/extra-large (US).

This is a **FLAME TREE** book
First published in 2009

Publisher and Creative Director: Nick Wells
Project Editor: Cat Emslie
Art Director: Mike Spender
Layout Design: Dave Jones
Digital Design and Production: Chris Herbert
Picture Research: Cat Emslie
Proofreader: Dawn Laker
Indexer: Helen Snaith

Special thanks to Megan Mizanty

09 11 13 12 10

1 3 5 7 9 10 8 6 4 2

This edition first published 2009 by
FLAME TREE PUBLISHING
Crabtree Hall, Crabtree Lane
Fulham, London SW6 6TY
United Kingdom

www.flametreepublishing.com

Flame Tree is part of The Foundry Creative Media Co. Ltd
© The Foundry Creative Media Co. Ltd

ISBN 978-1-84786-528-1

A CIP Record for this book is available from the British Library upon request

Printed in India

All pictures courtesy of The Foundry, except the following, which are courtesy of Shutterstock and © the following photographers: 1 & 56 Zaneta Baranowska;
3 & 60 Arkady; 4 & 18 Ioannis Ioannou; 5 & 76, 50b Rob Byron; 6t & 128 ulga; 6b & 176 Bochkarev Photography; 7 & 192, 68 najmu; 8t & 208, 63 Magdalena
Kucova; 8b & 224 Denis Miraniuk; 9 & 244, 44, 144 Viktor1; 10 Pete Saloutos; 11 wrangler; 12, 34 Diego Cervo; 13b, 38, 40, 52 Yuri Arcurs; 13t RedTC; 14b, 59
Rafa Irusta; 14t Alexei Novikov; 15 APaterson; 17 vgstudio; 20 Cre8tive Images; 21 GeoM; 22 Sinisa Botas; 23 Tyler Olson; 24 Jostein Hauge; 26 Serg64; 27
Workmans Photos; 29, 37 Stephen Coburn; 31 Christa DeRidder; 32 karen roach; 35 Marc Dietrich; 42b Ronen; 42t Baloncici; 45 Christopher S. Howeth; 46 Graca
Victoria; 48 mates; 49 Sally Scott; 50t Georgy Markov; 54, 98, 145, 148, 158, 161, 168, 170, 171 Monkey Business Images; 55 Paul Cowan; 57, 61
AGphotographer; 58 Fairybloom; 64 Claude Beaubien; 67 erperlstrom; 70 Roman Sigaev; 71 Liz Van Steenburgh; 73 NEIL ROY JOHNSON; 74 Carly Rose Hennigan;
78 yamix; 79, 91 Rob Marmion; 81 Gladskikh Tatiana; 83 Luis Castro; 85 Magdalena Bujak; 86 Brian Chase; 89 piotr adamski; 93 Tomasz Trojanowski; 95
boumen&japet; 97 Germany Feng; 99 sban; 101 Thomas M Perkins; 103 Carina Lochner; 105 Feng Yu; 107 Natalia Bratslavsky; 108 KariDesign; 110 spfotocz; 112
Spsergey; 114 Dmitry Melnikov; 116 Piotr Rzeszutek; 118 David Mzareulyan; 119 Tania Zbrodko; 122 Lori Sparkia; 123 Soyka; 124 Blazej Maksym; 127 terekhov
igor; 130 wikkie; 133 :: IntraClique :: LLC; 134 PeJo; 136 rj lerich; 139 LockStockBob; 141 Douglas Freer; 150 Neross; 151 Josh Resnick; 153 Pixelspieler; 155 sds-
studio; 157 Julija Sapic; 163 Stephanie Frey; 165 Sean Wandzilak; 167 Kiselev Andrey Valerevich; 172 Scott Rothstein; 174 Robyn Mackenzie; 175 HomeStudio

Food on a Budget
Meals for Beginners

DIANE & JON SUTHERLAND

Series Foreword: Tony Turnbull

**FLAME TREE
PUBLISHING**

Contents

Managing to shop on a budget begins before you even enter the grocery store. You need to decide on your menus for the week, plan your shop and choose where to shop, before you head out to find the best deals. You can stretch your budget even further by growing your own herbs and vegetables. You do not need an enormous amount of space to do this and it is rewarding. If you are a beginner shopper, this chapter will really help.

Kitchen Basics

Where can you find the cheapest, best quality cleaning products? In fact, you can make your own. Keeping your kitchen clean and hygienic is essential and there are tips galore in this chapter. What do you need to successfully run your kitchen? Is it really necessary to buy expensive labour-saving devices? It can be just as easy to do the jobs manually. What about storing your food and prolonging its life? Learn all this and more here.

All the basic techniques are here; you will find out how to deal with meat and poultry, fish, vegetables, rice and pasta. The wonders of one-pot meals are discussed, alongside advice on following recipes. The chapter even shows you how to make your own bread, cakes, pies, pasta and stock from scratch. Then find out how to stretch your food, use those meal leftovers and fridge remnants, and reduce your kitchen waste.

This chapter features a great selection of soups, starters and appetizers from around the world. When entertaining, you can really impress with Chinese Chicken Soup made from leftovers, or make your own delicious gnocchi with grilled cherry tomato sauce. You can even make your own tasty dill sauce to accompany hand-made beetroot ravioli. Your guests will never guess just how little it has cost you to put this delicious extra course together.

Recipes: Fish & Seafood

No need to be scared of cooking fish any more, with a great range of easy-to-follow and appealing recipes for fish dishes. Seafood is something even experienced cooks shy away from, but this chapter shows you how to create exotic Citrus Grilled Plaice or Coconut Fish Curry. If you prefer something a little more homely, try the fish pie, or fish and pasta dishes. The recipes avoid the more typically pricey fish – but anything can be found at a good price if you try.

Recipes: Meat & Poultry

For many, meat and poultry dishes are the ultimate main course. Find)out how to use mince, sausages, bacon and cheap meat and poultry cuts to produce taste sensations alongside olives, crispy-skinned potatoes, noodles, pasta and rice. Create your own exceptional Mexican, Thai, Chinese, Italian and traditional meat and poultry dishes to impress and tantalize the taste buds. No nonsense, no hassle, no problem, low-cost solutions for every occasion.

Recipes: Vegetables

Vegetables, as a main dish or as an accompaniment, they are all here. Span the globe and taste dishes from the four corners of the earth. Vegetables can be nourishing, wholesome and, above all, can be the cheapest element of a meal. From exotic curried potatoes with spinach to warm and satisfying vegetable and lentil casseroles, there is no fish, meat or poultry, so these recipes are great for vegetarians – but check the ingredients.

Recipes: Desserts & Sweet Treats 244

Food on a budget should not mean you forego dessert or the odd treat. This chapter shows you how to round off your meal with a flourish, with Lemon Surprise, Marbled Chocolate Tray Bake or Crunchy Rhubarb Crumble. These naughty but nice delights will not break the bank. Not only are they easy to achieve, but they cost very little. You will feel proud of yourself and rightly feel you have deserved the indulgence.

Index 254

Series Foreword

Last night I made a chorizo and chickpea casserole. I sweated some onions in a little olive oil, threw in the chopped-up Spanish sausage and, once it had released its golden, paprika-spiked juices, I added chicken stock, chickpeas and some sliced cabbage. It bubbled away happily for about twenty minutes, and then I finished it off with a squeeze of lemon juice, a bit of seasoning, and ate it with a crust of bread. It probably cost a total of three pounds and was utterly delicious, even if I do say so myself.

Did I do it to be cheap? Not at all — although the fact that it didn't break the bank was certainly a bonus. I did it because that is what proper cooking is about — taking a few raw ingredients and, through the alchemy of heat, creating a dish that is greater than the sum of its parts.

People get too hung up on price anyway. Budget cooking doesn't necessarily mean cheap cooking. It doesn't mean filling your fridge with two-for-ones or limp vegetables going cheap at the market. It's more a state of mind, of being aware of what food is costing you, and making the most of what you then buy. Sometimes I like to cook a beautiful steak or a whole sea bass, neither of which can be called cheap, but if I can wring maximum value out of them, it's money well spent.

Let's go back to that chorizo casserole. The most expensive element was the chorizo. I got mine from my local butcher so, while it wasn't authentically Spanish, it was half the price. I wouldn't serve it thinly sliced with an aperitif, but for throwing into a stew, it was well up to the job. Why pay extra if you aren't going to appreciate its nuances of flavour? Ditto the olive oil – only a fool fries with extra-virgin – save that for dressing a salad or finished dish.

The stock was home-made, using the carcass from a Sunday roast, plus the peelings from the leeks and carrots I served it with. That doesn't mean it was free, because to make a decent stock, you need to start with a decent, free range chicken. But it meant I could justify buying the more expensive bird, and enjoying its superior flavour, because I knew it would be giving me not one, but two meals.

So, spend your money where it counts, and plan ahead. These are the cornerstones of budget cooking. It's not about deprivation, but about that rather old-fashioned notion of good housekeeping. And finally, don't beat yourself up too much. I ended up using two cans of instant chickpeas, when I should really have soaked my own the night before. But really, pre-soaking chickpeas? Who's got time for that?

Tony Turnbull is food and drink editor of *The Times*

Introduction

Feeding yourself tasty home-cooked meals when on a budget can be a challenge. Fast food may *seem* to be a cheaper way, but it really is not and it certainly is not as healthy. In fact, healthy foods can often be cheaper than most junk foods. All you need to do is to make some straightforward changes to cut down on how much you spend on food. Simple things like switching to more filling wholegrain bread or drinking water instead of carbonated drinks will be a start.

It is Nothing New

There has always been a great food divide. In the past, a huge proportion of the population could often not afford to eat. Unfortunately, this is still the case in many developing countries. Compared to the rich, people on lower incomes tend to eat less well, but strangely they may pay more for their food. They eat poorer quality food and, as a result, suffer from diet-related ill health. It is all about dietary imbalance or undernourishment. Even in developed countries, five per cent of adults cannot afford to eat fresh fruit daily. One in twenty mothers go without food so that their children can eat. The problem is that those buying food on a budget will often buy the wrong food from the wrong places.

Wartime Restrictions

Many of the tips and tricks that we now take for granted were learned in far more difficult times; how to stretch food, how to make use of food that might otherwise be wasted. Many countries suffered from rationing during the Second World War for example, as basic items like butter, meat, poultry, eggs, fruit and vegetables were scarce and what was available was expensive. In fact, in Britain, for example, the use of ration books actually improved the nation's health because it brought in a balanced diet that had all of the necessary vitamins. People were encouraged to grow their own foods and even raise their own animals. Nothing could afford to be wasted. In today's world, we see rocketing global prices for staple foods. Although there is no rationing, this puts an enormous strain on household budgets.

Food Shortages

Luckily, with the exception of a few unfortunate countries and generations in recent years, famines are far less common than they once were. Over the centuries, famines have swept across the world, changing our diets – often for ever. In the so-called potato famine in Ireland in the nineteenth century, disease, starvation and emigration reduced the population by a quarter. Whilst this was an extreme case, there have tended to be food shortages due to crop failures, natural disasters, war or health scares. Whilst much is being done to try to ensure that worldwide food production continues to reach record levels, global food shortages still threaten the lives of millions. As a result, these food shortages impact on the developed world, pushing up prices and making it even more difficult to eat within a reasonable budget.

Frugal Cooks of the Past

Our ancestors were always aware that they could not guarantee where they might find their next meal. They did not live in a time where food was plentiful, easy and cheap to purchase and almost inexhaustible. They wasted nothing, using animal bones to make stock and form the basis of another meal. No part of the animal was ever wasted. They would have to eat seasonal fruit and vegetables and when they could not do this they had to rely on produce that they had preserved for themselves, having put it into storage for the leaner winter months. Preserving and storing food remains an important part of keeping within a food budget, stocking up when supply is plentiful and prices are low and then using them when supplies dwindle and prices rise.

Frugal Cooks Today

We too can be frugal cooks, by organizing ourselves and our kitchens. Buying in-season produce is a great way of eating on a budget. Most canned fruits and vegetables are cheaper than out-of-season fresh produce and on balance they are no less healthy than fresh, as the way they are processed means that they do not lose as many  nutrients as you might expect. Growing your own vegetables is another great idea. You can easily grow half a dozen tomato plants in the tiniest of spaces. It will give you fresh produce all through the summer. Steering clear of ready-packaged food saves money. It will not only cost you more but you will also be eating a less healthy diet by putting those ready meals into your shopping trolley – although some manufacturers are starting to cater to the worries about nutrition and health, the main problems with ready meals are still their high levels of fat, salt and additives. Be in control of what goes into your food!

Preparation for Perfection

Preparing before you grocery shop will save you money. Planning out your meals each week before you go to the grocery store, checking sale advertisements, clipping out coupons and looking out for bargains all helps. You will find all of the necessary hints and tips on how to prepare for shopping on a budget in our first chapter, which even tells you how to make the best use of all of those marketing ploys grocery stores use to try to influence your purchases.

The Smooth Transition

Switching over to the low budget and healthier approach can be an exciting adventure. For the first time, you can prepare everything that you eat and learn about the ingredients. You can quickly pick up the basic techniques and understand what goes into every meal. Make it a joint venture and go on the healthy, low budget journey together with your friends or partner. It may seem like an impossible task, but practice will make perfect. We can learn so much from our ancestors. Our times may be as difficult and our budgets may be as tight, but many of the tricks and solutions that they came up with when they had to work on a budget are as good today as they were in past years. Even those without a garden can grow their own herbs and vegetables, we can all learn how to prolong the life of the food we buy and cut down on the amount of waste and cost.

Back to Basics

As a beginner, this book assumes that you have limited experience in buying for yourself, organizing your kitchen or cooking for yourself and others. All of the key tips, techniques and short cuts are here to help you, from how to fillet a fish, prepare vegetables and understand a recipe. We even show you how to create your own cleaning products that will keep your kitchen spotless and hygienic. We identify every piece of kitchen equipment that you really need and tell you the ones you can easily manage without.

Recipes Galore

There are also dozens of great budget-minded, flavoursome recipes that will give you a taste of what you can achieve. None of them requires you to have overly expensive ingredients, complicated and costly equipment or a huge amount of time to spare. And remember, you can always adapt them to your needs or your cupboard! The recipes are all designed to impress both your own taste buds and any fortunate guest who might sit at your table. Cooking is something to be enjoyed and part of that excitement is in the preparation and the presentation of a freshly cooked and wholesome, nutritious meal that you have made with your own hands.

An Essential Guide

This book provides you with everything you need to know, from when and where to shop, how to get the best prices, what to buy and when to buy it. There are handy tips on how to grow your own, bake your own and make your own. You can see how to make bread and pasta from scratch, cakes and pastries, as well as delicious pies. But the book does not stop there. Not only are there all the techniques you will need to know about cooking meat, fish, poultry, vegetables, rice and other delicious ingredients, but also how to stretch those meals and make the best out of the ingredients you have to hand. Nothing goes to waste: you can recycle leftovers, use up vegetable trimmings, switch ingredients in recipes and learn how to reduce or increase the quantities in a recipe to match the numbers at your dinner table.

Over to You

Everything in this book is designed to be as practical as possible. We show you how to do it, so it is up to you to try. There are bargains to be had, there is a solution to every problem, there are short cuts that will save you time, money and effort, there are ways to avoid disasters, there are ways to use things; everyday household items that you may never have thought of before. You will not need to scrape your leftovers into the bin any more, or be disappointed with what you have finally put on to your plate. Now is the time to make the positive switch to food on a budget. It is not about being mean, it is about being careful and what is more, it is about being healthier too. Try out some of the basic techniques for yourself and find out how easy it is to buy, prepare, cook and enjoy food on a budget today.

Shopping
for
Beginners

PACKED WITH
MONEY
SAVING
IDEAS & TIPS

Planning to Shop

Recent increases in food prices have meant that most families' weekly shopping bills have risen by around 20 per cent. Prices for all staples – rice, pasta, bread, eggs and butter – have reached record levels. And prices could rise by around 15 per cent year-on-year in the foreseeable future. Working out a budget for your food shopping is just part of a wider strategy. Prioritizing your food shopping depends on all of your other expenditure, but the best place to start is well before you go into a food store.

Preparation, Preparation, Preparation

Preparing before you shop stops the store from steering your trolley. Stores are designed to make us impulse spend. They spend millions trying to seduce us into buying more than we actually need and buying brand names when there are perfectly good and cheaper substitutes available. Preparation is the first step to take control and shop on a budget, the best start to put you back in charge of your own shopping.

Change Your Mindset

Preparation begins with changing your mindset:

 Stop thinking: 'How can I get what I want at the cheapest price?'

 Start thinking: 'I've got this amount to spend, what is the most I can get with it?'

Checking the Cupboards

You cannot afford to throw food away; it is just like throwing money away. The first thing to do is to make total use of everything you have in your store cupboard. And do not forget all that fresh food that is likely to rot in the bottom of the refrigerator. We throw out a third of all the

food we buy. For every ten million people, that is over a million tonnes of food every year thrown out. The average couple throws out over £400/US$550 of good food every year, while the average family with children throws out over £600/US$830 of perfectly edible food each year. In the UK, it has been worked out that every day are thrown out:

 1.3 million pots of unopened yoghurt
 5,500 whole chickens
 440,000 ready meals

Cost of Waste

The cost does not end there: it costs the economy millions to deal with the food waste. If we stopped throwing out food, the drop in carbon dioxide emissions would be like reducing the number of cars by 20 per cent. We do not just throw out rotten food; 20 per cent of it is still in date.

Take a Stock Check

How many different places in your home do you store food? Food is tucked away not just in the kitchen store cupboards or in the refrigerator or freezer. What about the food you have stashed:

 in the garage?

in your second fridge or freezer?

in those cupboards you do not often use?

Are you throwing food away just to make room for new food? Stop now! It is costing you a fortune! It is not just the space you are wasting, or the energy to run those extra fridges and freezers. It is the money you have spent and the meals you could have enjoyed.

Do a Larder Audit

Rather than throwing that food away, do a regular audit every few weeks. Check the dates and then make sure you use it before you lose it. Take it all out of the cupboard, fridge or freezer and start to arrange it by meals. If you cannot think of something to do with the cans, bottles or food you have found, try a website like www.cookingbynumbers.com. It shows you what you can make from those ingredients and gives you the recipe too.

Knowing What You've Got

Half the battle is knowing what is already in your freezer, fridge, pantry, spice rack and all those other hidden places. You will already have a long list of ingredients. They do not need to be on your shopping list. Making an inventory aims to give you direction and discipline. It will help you plan your shopping so you only have to buy what you really need and not what you think you need.

Plan Ahead

Now you have listed your stored food and you know how long you have got left to use it, your shopping can focus on what is missing. Think about the week ahead. When are you going to eat the food you have found and what do you need to add to it to make a meal? This should be your starting point. Now you can begin to make your shopping list.

Making a List

Shopping on a budget does not mean having to make compromises. In fact, shopping on a budget and making the best use of the food that you have not only saves you money but also helps you to eat healthily. We will see that the menu is at the heart of saving money on groceries and the menus are made up of recipes. If you can control the recipes then you can control your costs.

Menu Plan

A menu plan is a list of meals that you are going to prepare and serve over the course of the week. All the food that you are going to buy will be based on the menus, so your menu plan is your shopping starting point – it will provide you with your master shopping list. The menu needs to give you a good variety – budget shopping does not need to compromise any health requirements. The menu plan needs to be:

 healthy
 nutritious
 well balanced

Leftovers as Part of the Menu Plan

Planning to create what could be food waste may sound mad. But think about the possibilities of leftovers when you plan your menus: uneaten vegetables can be mashed in with potatoes for a bit of variety, and uneaten chicken can be turned into a delicious curry the next day. There are economies to be made by buying oversized chickens and joints of meat because they are the ones that are discounted first through lack of sales. If you do not intend to eat the leftovers straight away you could also freeze them.

The Master Shopping List

A master shopping list will save you time. You will not have to create one over and over again. Do the work now; it will only take a few minutes.

Regular purchases: The first step is to make a list of items that you always buy. This is the most time consuming part.

A reminder: Look at your old store receipts; they will remind you about what you buy and how often you buy it.

Categorization: Sort the list by categories. You could do this by sorting them by store aisle provided you are intending to use the same store. Sorting will mean that you will not miss anything out and it will save you time too.

Technological List

If you have a computer and a spreadsheet package, this is ideal to create your list. You can print one off each time you shop and cross off all the things you do not need. The other great thing with a spreadsheet is that you can include the price you paid last time to monitor price changes. It will also help you to estimate your shopping bill before you even leave for the store. It can also be the basis of another strategy: shopping around. Not all the bargains will be in one store.

Using the List

The list is your master shopping list but it is something more than that. You can use it all week. Fix it to the refrigerator and when something is used up from your master list, highlight it. This will mean that you replace it on your next shopping trip. If you have included the prices on your list, everyone in the household will see exactly how much has just been spent by using that item. It might make them think.

Shop Smart List

You might have designed your list with one store in mind but that does not mean that you cannot buy items somewhere other than your regular store. You don't need to go to discount stores or health food stores every week, so you might want to categorize the items you do buy from them separately. You might also want to leave some blank lines at the end of your list. Sometimes there will be special purchases to be made.

Price Books

A price book can really help you save money. Basically, you use it to record the prices of the items you buy frequently. This will help you to recognize when a food-store bargain is a cost saver and when it is not. You will know the price you paid in the past and it will help avoid costly mistakes. It can help you save money by knowing how much you should be paying for the items that you use the most frequently.

Your Buying History

Why should the store have the advantage? If you have a customer loyalty card then every purchase that you have made is logged and in the store's database. They know what you buy, how often you buy it and how much you paid for it. The trouble is, *you* do not always know. But now you can with a price book. You can log:

 when you bought

where you bought

how many you bought

what price you paid

How Does a Price Book Help?

You can now see that the prices have been going up and down. It might be time to see if you can get your frequent purchases cheaper somewhere else. Better still, there might be a time of the year when you could stock up because the price always drops then. You could also discover that if you bought in bulk you could save even more money. Businesses use this technique all the time. They can spot a good deal and that is when they stock up.

Creating Your Price Book

There is no hard and fast way to do this and it depends how much detail you want to include. At a minimum, your price book needs to include your regular purchases. People who create price books use:

Large notebooks: Each item is given its own page. The price charged in a particular store on a particular day is listed. Each time you look in a different store you can log their price.

 Small pocket notebooks: This is the most convenient as you visit various stores. You can organize the products in alphabetical order and jot down the lowest price that you find.

 Computer spreadsheet: Not exactly the most convenient unless you are really high-tech. But you can make instant spreadsheet updates and keep a track on prices.

 Index cards: An ideal convenient and sortable system. It also means you can pull out the cards to match your menus and your master list and take them along with you.

The Price Book Really Works

It stops you falling for deceptive advertising in store. Suppose you see something you usually buy marked down to half price. It looks like a bargain but when you look at your price book you can see that only a month ago this half price was the regular price. Your price book can become your own personal record of the best deals you have ever had. You will begin to see the patterns that the manufacturers and the stores use. Use it regularly and keep track of the prices. It is really an excellent tool to help you save money. You can also use the price book to see how much your favourite recipes cost. You can price up all the ingredients and see if there is a cheaper alternative. Why not switch from chopped tomatoes to whole tomatoes and chop them yourself?

Coupons and Vouchers

Another way that stores aim to steer your shopping trolley is to tempt you to buy things you would not normally consider. They offer you coupons and money-off vouchers. Stores call this 'capture and exploit'. First, they aim to bring new customers in to their store with their discount vouchers and codes. This is the capture part. For regular customers, they aim to exploit impulse spending by offering promotions on what are really luxury items. You can use these promotions to turn the tables on the stores.

Coupons - Are They New?

Billions are offered by manufacturers and stores in coupon savings. Coupons are as old as the hills and in fact the first grocery coupon was created in 1894, when you could exchange one for a free glass of Coca-Cola. Things have moved on a lot since then. The first coupons began appearing on the internet in the middle of the 1990s. In the US, shoppers use over four billion coupons a year, saving them nearly the same amount in dollars. Over 77 per cent of households use coupons. Weirdly, the more you earn, the more likely you are to use coupons.

You Don't Need Coupons to Save

We are going to look at all the places you can find coupons and how to manage them. But you do not actually need to have coupons to save money. All you need to do is to plan in an effective way. Later, we are going to look at those 2-for-1 sales and all of those seasonal offers. They can offer you as good and sometimes better savings than a fistful of coupons.

Where to Find Coupons

There are coupons, vouchers and codes everywhere. If you have a store loyalty card, you can often find a coupon at the end of your receipt, personalized for your own buying habits. This is one of the best ones, but only if you really need it and it can offer you a good deal. Wherever you find coupons, it is important to remember that they are only any good if you use them at the right time. Most of them will have expiry dates, so it is easy to miss the offer. But the golden rule is never to use coupons on something you do not need just because the store is offering it at a cheaper price.

Hunting for Coupons

Grocery coupons are not just in magazines. There are whole websites devoted to them, with hundreds of links and special codes that have worked for other people. Some stores will even accept coupons and vouchers for products that they are not even designed for. Sometimes you can use a voucher for a box of cereal and actually get that money off your total shopping bill without even having bought cereal. Store policies differ; some will not accept coupons if you have not made that product purchase. But some stores will accept up to £10/US$14 worth of these coupons. There is no harm in trying, but you need to be upfront and see if they will accept them.

Paper Sources

Newspapers and magazines are a great place to begin your hunt for those coupons and coupon inserts. Inside your newspapers and magazines, you will find clip-out coupons on advertisements. There are also flyers, either from a store or a manufacturer, that you can use. If you are unsure when the coupons will appear, find out when your favourite newspaper has a food section. It is usually at the weekends and that is where you will find the bulk of the coupons.

On-pack Sources

Manufacturers call them self-liquidating premiums. This is when you will find a coupon on or in the product itself. Some you have to peel off or clip out to give you savings on your next purchase. These are designed to keep you loyal to a brand, so use them sparingly and only if the brand still offers you value. Some are designed to cross-sell other brands that the manufacturer offers. The big manufacturers offer a huge range of different food and household items, so buying some washing powder might give you money off that manufacturer's coffee.

Online Coupons

This is the big growth area. But you need to be organized to take advantage. There are
hundreds of websites where you can get printable grocery coupons, so you no longer have
to rely on offers that are pushed through your letterbox or in your newspaper or magazines.
In the US, you can use www.smartsource.com or www.valpak.com, and in the UK,
www.vouchercodes.com or www.couponwatch.co.uk. There are hundreds of others and every
country has its own range of websites.

Big Discounts

Discount vouchers are used by plenty of stores to try to capture new customers. This is particularly true if you buy online and have your groceries delivered. But you can also present these vouchers at a store. Why not switch if you need to stock up and the store's prices are competitive? You could save as much as 20 per cent or more as a new customer. To make full use of this system, you will need to shift your buying from one store to another. Check to see what counts as being a new customer. You may qualify if you have not made a purchase from them for a few months.

Rain-check Vouchers

Some stores will hand out special vouchers that you can use when their special offer products are out of stock. After all, that is why you visited the store in the first place. If you see empty shelves or freezer cabinets where a genuine special offer should have been and you had intended to buy them, head straight for the Customer Service desk. Ask for a voucher. You can then take advantage of the special offer when stocks are replenished, even though the special offer period might have ended.

Special Coupons

Another way stores handle situations when their special offers have run out is to give you a coupon so that you can buy the same product, but a different brand. You will be able to buy it at the special offer price even though that brand is not discounted. You will usually have to use the coupon on the day. Once again, make your way to the Customer Service desk and even if they do not offer rain-check coupons, they might offer this alternative.

Problem Vouchers

Some stores will offer money vouchers, which you can set against your shopping bill. These are given out if you have had a problem with something you have bought from the store; maybe one egg of a dozen was bad. Sometimes they will give them out if special offer products are out of stock. They are usually given out at the discretion of the store manager.

Store Clubs and Loyalty Cards

Many of the chain stores have their own exclusive clubs. Wine clubs are an ideal example. Club members get special money-off vouchers and not just wine-related ones. If you sign up and stay on their mailing list, you get special offers posted to you. Loyalty cards are an excellent way of gaining money-off vouchers. You usually get one point for every pound or dollar you spend. It can mean as much as five per cent off all your grocery spending because they will send you money-off coupons and sheets of special deals. You can save money and get extra points at the same time.

Coupons - What's in It for Them?

Stores want to manipulate what you buy, how much you buy and when you buy it. Stores are not charities, so they are not giving away something for nothing. Maybe these items are massively overstocked? Maybe they have got a great deal from their supplier or maybe they just want to tempt you to get into new purchasing habits? If you try something new on the strength of a coupon offer, then there is a good chance you will continue to buy it when the offer ends. By then, of course, the price will have gone up, but you will be hooked.

Coupons - What's in It for You?

If you play the coupon game right, you can make great savings on things you would be buying anyway. It needs organization, like anything, and you also need to be able to spot what is a genuine deal compared to a marketing ploy. A coupon might just bring the price of something down to the regular price charged in other stores. Or it might be a genuine price saving that no one else can match. Play the coupon game to win but remember you need to be in charge of the when, the where and the amount you buy and not them.

Organizing Your Coupons

There is no point in collecting coupons if you do not use them. How frustrating is it to find a coupon for one of your regular purchases only to see that it is out of date? How frustrated would you be to be standing in the checkout line and realize you have a coupon but cannot find it? You need to organize the coupons. Some people use:

- **Envelopes**: These are ideal if you do not use lots of coupons.

- **Recipe boxes**: Place the coupons beside your favourite recipes in your menu planner.

- **Shoeboxes**: Make yourself some cardboard dividers and categorize your coupons.

- **Binders**: Get some plastic pockets and categorize your coupons.

- **Concertina file**: Organize your coupons alphabetically or by their 'valid until' date.

Winning the Coupon Battle

Sometimes, stores will send you a coupon or vouchers that will double either your savings or your customer loyalty points. To tempt you away, other stores may be prepared to match the savings. The matching store may even have lower prices to begin with, so you could not only double your savings but you could treble them by seeing if they will play ball and take your coupons.

Discount Vouchers and Promotion Codes

Voucher codes are a great way to save money, particularly if you are shopping online. Sometimes they are called e-vouchers or discount codes. All they are, are special codes that will give you a discount or money off from the retailer. You need to be quick because most of the vouchers only last for a few days. There are websites that specialize in listing all of the current codes (some were mentioned earlier), but the stores themselves may email you with gift or claim codes, just to tempt you to shop. Do not forget that free delivery (usually when you spend over a certain amount) saves you the transport costs of getting to and from a store.

How to Use Discount and Voucher Codes

Remember:

 Why they exist: The codes are used by the store or manufacturer to drive up sales on a particular product.

 Same old: All they are is an adaptation of the traditional way to offer special discounts.

Variety: At any time, there will be thousands of valid codes.

Choose websites carefully: Make sure that the voucher codes website you use is regularly added to and updated.

When to use the code: You will need to note down the code and enter it at the checkout stage when buying online.

Who can use the codes: Usually there are no limitations on who can use the codes but often it is only one code per household.

When to Shop

When humans were hunter-gatherers, they would go shopping for their food with their spear in their hand when they felt hungry. Sometimes, they ran into food sources they could not handle and came off worse. Now we have got superstores and we can still come off worse if we go shopping when we are hungry. It is the golden rule: never shop for food if your stomach is rumbling! If you go shopping when you are hungry, you will spend at least 10 per cent more on your groceries.

Times to Shop

Choosing the right time to shop is obviously down to personal preference and circumstances, but here are some golden rules:

- ☑ **Vulnerable times**: Try not to shop after work or on pay day or just before a public holiday.

- ☑ **In advance of need**: Shop before you run out and not when you desperately need something, otherwise you will end up paying a premium price for convenience.

Buy in season: Learn the sales cycle and buy items when they are cheap and plentiful and not when they are out of season.

 Buy local: Go for home grown and not imported products. This means knowing when fresh produce is in season.

Monthly staples: Do a monthly bulk shopping trip for staples like canned tomatoes, flour, sugar and coffee.

Frequent trips for near-perishing items: Make frequent trips to the store if you are aiming to use products that are close to their 'sell-by' or 'use-by' dates, but do not make impulse buys while you are there.

Suit Yourself - Shop Solo

A partner or friend can be useful for trolley steering and for loading bags, but they can also cloud your judgement. Now you have your master shopping list and you are focused on what you need rather than what you want, shopping on your own can stop you making those impulse buys. With many stores open 24 hours a day to catch shift workers and those who work unsociable hours, pick a time to suit you. Evenings are a good time to pick up reduced groceries, particularly perishable items. Research has shown that weekday mornings are the quietest for food shopping. A less busy store means you will forget less, with the added bonus of getting less irritated.

Give Yourself Time

You might think that if you have plenty of time to walk around and browse the store that you will end up buying more. This is not true if you are disciplined. If you are not rushed, you won't forget things, you won't snatch up things that you do not need and, above all, you won't miss the best deals. You will have a chance to check the price per ounce or per gram and compare like for like. This will help you find the best value for money. You can compare brands and you can also compare different types of food and consider substitutes. When something is on sale, buy lots of it. Look out for those regular purchases that are marked down temporarily and stock up. You will then have enough until the price is marked down again in a few weeks' time.

How Often to Shop

Every trip to the store will probably cost you money and time. For most people, a monthly bulk shop for staples, backed up by a weekly shop for fresh produce, is far more economical than daily trips to the store. This might present a problem if you do not have your own transport. But it does not mean you need to shop just within walking distance, or where public transport will conveniently drop you. There are still plenty of options and they do not have to be the most expensive ones, like the local convenience stores that are often more expensive than the superstores. A great option is to buy online. The store may charge you for delivery, but this might be cheaper than taking a bus or using a taxi cab. Weigh up your options, but online shopping stops impulse buys too.

Where to Shop

Humans are inquisitive creatures; they love to explore and to find things out. Explore your local shopping environment and you will find far more places than you could possibly imagine. Do not forget that all of the stores, market stalls and other outlets are competing with one another for your money. Each of them will want to tempt you in, to convince you to buy and to sell you things you did not know you needed at prices you should not be paying.

Places to Shop

It can be daunting; there are wholesalers, cash and carry, hypermarkets, superstores, outdoor and indoor markets, convenience stores, discount superstores and online stores. Expect to see the best-known brands in most of these, but between these smart displays of household names there are brands you may never have heard of and they are just as good. The more you look, the more you will find and the more options, the greater the chance to save money.

Superstores

For most people, the superstore is the major place for the monthly and weekly shops. There is a bewildering range of products available. There are luxury brands, regular day-to-day brands, and discount brands, like the store's own label products. Many of them are now offering 'real value' brands. Some of them can easily compete with the wholesalers and with the discounters' prices, but shop selectively and do not get sucked in. Use the choice they offer to your advantage:

✅ **Top brand names**: Buy brands if you have coupons or they are on special offer.

✅ **Other brands**: Buy lesser-known brands if they offer better value.

✅ **Own brand**: Buy unbranded or the supermarket's own brands if they are staples.

✅ **'Basic' lines**: Do buy 'real value' brands as they can save you a lot – but do not buy them in bulk until you have tried them and checked out their quality.

Wholesalers

Some wholesalers do not welcome consumers. But most of them are not foolish enough to turn away a sale. You may need to buy a case of canned tomatoes or a dozen bottles of olive oil. If you are going to be using them anyway and the price is right, why not buy them in bulk? Getting them home is an issue but consider that you may not have to buy any more for a year. A great way to shop and save at wholesalers is to buy a case and split it with friends or family. That way, the savings are shared and they can make the bulk purchase next time to share with you.

Discount Stores

Discount stores are full of products that you have either never heard of or are well-known brands that are overstocked. They want you to buy in bulk. They reward you for buying in bulk. The choices might not be as great as a regular store, but that is not the point. This is where to buy your staples once a month. It is also a great way to practically downshift. If you have been buying branded goods, why not downshift to a cheaper brand? We look at practical downshifting when we see how to get the best prices.

Markets

Indoor and outdoor fresh-produce markets offer an exciting but enticingly different way of shopping. Most neighbourhoods have markets, either weekday ones or at the weekend. One of the best times to hit these markets is towards the end of trading. The stallholders will not be looking forward to boxing up their displays and carrying them to their trucks and vans. They may be happy to do a deal. This is a discount paradise and a great way to buy your healthy fresh fruit and vegetables. Market stalls will also have discounted brand names and other brands you may never have heard of, with canned, bottled or other items with long 'use by' dates. These are overstocks too, and can often be real bargains.

Convenience Stores

Your local convenience store cannot possibly compete with the discounters, either on price or on range available. But this does not mean that they will not have bargains. Do not use convenience stores for your regular weekly shops, but be prepared to step inside and see if they have special offers and promotions that even the big stores cannot match. Do not forget the other major advantage – they are not called convenience stores for nothing; getting to them may not cost you anything, so the odd penny or cent here and there may not matter.

Online Shopping

Many of the major superstores and other businesses have online grocery shopping websites. A lot of them try to make the website as close to shopping for real in their store as possible. This is not just to make you feel more comfortable, or to give you a chance to experience the real thing in a virtual world. They want to use the same tricks online as they do in their aisles. So watch out! The other major thing to remember about online shopping is that someone else is choosing your groceries:

- ☑ **forget finding the one with the longest 'use by' date**
- ☑ **forget finding the undamaged package**
- ☑ **forget finding unblemished fruit and vegetables**
- ☑ **forget wanting a particular brand**
- ☑ **forget wanting a particular flavour or perfume**

Or, rather, you can specify most of the above, but your personal shopper is trained to substitute if products are out of stock. And do not forget to factor in any delivery charge that the superstore might make.

Online Alternatives

You do not need to make all your purchases from a superstore's website. There are plenty of online businesses that can deliver food to your door. Many of them will be specialists, such as:

- organic foods
- regional specialities
- natural foods
- cultural specialities
- dietary specialists
- food specialists, such as olive oil sellers

Bear in mind that the prices may be slightly higher and there is still a delivery charge to consider. But if you buy in bulk the prices can be lower and they can waive the delivery charges.

Marketing Tricks to Resist

Do not trust your senses! As soon as you walk into a store, you will be assailed with the smell of food, the sight of food, even the sound of food and packaging and you will be tempted to touch and experience the sensations. Everything is designed to manipulate your senses so that you will spend more money. So that is why another golden rule is to always shop after you have eaten. All the stores want you to buy more than you really need. If you can really appreciate this, then you will only walk out with what you need instead of what they want to sell you.

Smell

Have you noticed that many of the stores have their own bakeries? Have you noticed that you can smell what they are baking all around the store? It is enticing isn't it? But it is deliberate too. If you will not have eaten before you shop and you think you are going to be tempted when you smell freshly baked bread or glistening sugar-topped warm doughnuts, then drink a couple of glasses of water before you head for the store. It is easier to resist if you fool your body into believing your stomach is full.

Sight

Does the layout of the store annoy you? Why are they always moving your staples to different aisles? And why are they placed at the bottom of the shelves, making them hard for you to find? It is because they want you to look at everything. It is why what they want you to buy is at eye level. High priced items and brand names are conveniently located. Grocery stores know that by placing expensive products at eye level, you are more likely to buy them. Look up and down – the better value products are above or below the eye line.

Pretty Boxes

Reds and yellows – they are the colours that attract the buyer. They are intended to attract your attention. Ignore them and keep focused. Does a bigger box mean that there is more inside? Absolutely not; the packaging rarely has anything to do with the quantity that is inside. Many stores now have the price by weight, making it easier for you to make comparisons. But these are often printed on small tickets on the shelves and they are not conveniently placed either.

Temptation!

Watch out for those checkout aisles. While you are waiting in line to pay, there is nowhere to hide. Stores know they have a captive audience and whatever is placed by the checkouts is designed for those impulse buys that you need to avoid. One way of getting around this is to only ever shop during off-peak hours. You can get through the aisles quickly and avoid temptation. This is the store's last chance to influence your buying behaviour and they will try anything. Tempting confectionery, brightly coloured packages and 'must have' gadgets: ignoring them can be harder than you think.

Loss Leaders

Loss leaders are heavily discounted items that are publicized to attract you into the store. The store will be making little or no profit on them. But this is not because the store wants to save you money. They know that if you come in to buy the discounted items, you will end up buying other things too. Loss leaders can be discounted by more than 25 per cent off the normal price. Buy-one-get-one-frees are prime examples. Do not forget that you might have a coupon that you can combine with a loss leader deal. It could mean that you could save 75 per cent of the price or even get it for nothing!

When is a Sale Not a Sale?

Tempted by the word 'sale'? What does it really mean? Is it a real discount? Did they really sell it for that price? This is where your price book can save you from being fooled. The advertising might proclaim 50 per cent off, but your price book confirms that it has never been the price they claim is the normal retail price. You need to focus on the price of the product and not what the advertising is trying to tell you. Above all, if you were not planning to buy that item because you do not really need it, then whatever price you pay is not a bargain.

Get the Best Prices

We all need to buy groceries and we all have to eat. But there are ways to save money when you buy groceries without compromising on quality or nutritional value. If you look hard enough, you will always find the best deals. It may take a little bit of investment in time and money to get the full benefit of the best prices that are out there waiting for you. It is not about being cheap; it is about being sensible.

How to Get the Best Deals

We all know that the grocery store bill can be one of the biggest expenses, but it is incredibly easy to shrink that bill. Do not forget the useful points already discussed:

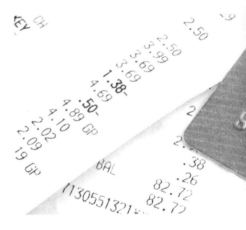

- **Discipline**: Use your willpower in the store – stick to your list and do not get tempted or impulse buy.

- **Planning**: Plan your meals ahead and make a list.

- **Coupons**: Sort out those coupons and take them along.

- **Wise sales buys**: If a sale is on and it is one of your staples, buy as much as you can afford.

- **Bulk buying**: Sometimes buy in bulk, but remember it only works if it is non-perishable, frozen or for a large family or event.

Accurate comparisons: When comparing, price everything per ounce or gram rather than per unit.

Wise brand buys: Compromise on brand names.

Rewards: Use your loyalty card.

Less stress: Shop on a weekday morning if you can.

Do not tempt the tummy: Never shop when you are hungry.

Solo shop: Try to shop alone.

Brand Names and Own Label

Manufacturers and stores have spent billions on convincing us that brand names are best. What we are buying is the most expensive version of a grocery item. If you are buying a premium brand, then downshift to a manufacturer's brand. If you are buying that brand already, then you could downshift to the store's own brand. If you are already buying the store's own brand, then consider downshifting to a no-frills or value brand. Do not assume that the value brand is inferior. The packaging may look more basic but in a lot of cases it is made in exactly the same factory as the gourmet version.

Save Yourself at Least 15 Per Cent a Year

By downshifting, an average household could save themselves hundreds of pounds/dollars a year. Try it. The next time you go to a store, downshift by one brand level. There are even websites to help you make the comparison before you go to the store. You can compare prices across levels and down levels. If you dropped one brand level on everything, then you could stand to cut your grocery bill by a third. In some cases, this could mean as much as over £/$100 a week for an average family.

Testing With Your Mouth, Not Your Eyes

Trust us, it is all psychological. The manufacturers and stores have hypnotized us. We assume that because the packaging is nicer and the price is higher that it tastes better. It doesn't always. In experiments, professional chefs have cooked three-course meals, one using regular ingredients and the other using downshifted ingredients. In blind taste tests, people preferred the downshifted versions. You can really make enormous savings without noticing the difference in your mouth but seeing the difference in your bank balance.

I Deserve Better!

It may come as a surprise, but some lower-cost alternatives can actually be better for you. They will have fewer expensive additives like colourings and flavourings or thickeners. So there is no real fear that downshifting means compromising on nutrition. Do not forget that, when you cook, the taste comes from how you cook that food and what you might add to it. We will look at some great cooking tips and techniques in our 'Basic Techniques' section. You can make up any loss of taste with your own time and cooking skills.

Tasty Own Brands

Is there any real difference between heavily promoted brand names and store own brands? Most of them are nutritionally identical. There are small differences that are deliberately added so that they do not taste exactly the same. Many of them taste so similar that most people will never notice the difference. Taste for yourself. Try downshifting and you will find that most of the own brands are just like the brand names, except they are in disguise.

Bulk Buying

Do not be daunted by this prospect; it does not mean that you need to order a truck load, or even fill a spare room, your garage or your store cupboards. Bulk buying can work and wholesalers often have great prices. However, there is no point in buying in bulk if you end up throwing out the food before you can eat it. A great way around this is to buy in bulk with friends and family and share out the case of canned fruit or baked beans. You can apply bulk buying to individuals and to couples too:

 Cook some, freeze some: Buy family-sized packages of meat, cook some now and put the rest in the freezer.

 Cook in bulk: It is just as easy to cook a large pan of soup or stew as it is a small one. Then, freeze your leftovers and eat them later. This works great with casseroles, for example.

 Frozen juice: Buy fresh fruit and vegetables in bulk when they are at the height of their season. Get the juicer out and freeze the fresh juice. Make soups and pot roasts, or parboil and freeze the vegetables.

Do You Trust Sell-by Dates?

Everyone is worried that buying in bulk means that you will end up throwing away the food because of short sell-by dates. You should not take risks, and you should certainly throw away:

 Cooked meats: Throw these away the day after their sell-by date unless you are planning to re-cook them thoroughly.

 Soft cheeses: There is a listeria threat here – it is very unpleasant and not worth the risk. The same goes for pâtés.

The following might not be at their best, but you could continue to eat them for up to two weeks after their sell-by date:

 Most eggs: But if the eggs smell bad when cracked open, throw them out! To test an egg's freshness, place the egg in a glass of cold water: if it sinks to a completely horizontal position, it is very fresh; if it tilts up slightly or to a semi-horizontal position, it could be up to a week old but is still perfectly usable; if it floats into a vertical position, then it is stale.

 Poultry and other raw meat: But make sure it is piping hot and thoroughly cooked when you serve it.

Milk: Even if it is sour, it won't hurt you and you can use it to make sauces.

Bread: Most is treated with an anti-fungal agent but you can scrape off the mould and toast it safely.

Don't Throw Away Those Antique Foods!

If a can or jar is not damaged or rusty, then food like baked beans can last for years. Hard cheeses will last for months. Lots of frozen food will last for months too, but the flavour will slowly deteriorate. Most dry food, like rice and pasta, will last for years, but once they are exposed to the moisture in the air, they will begin to taste stale, so they need to be kept airtight. Really, it is all down to common sense. Touch, smell and sample and cut down on unnecessary waste. Labels are contradictory and the use-by date is not an exact science.

Store Deals

We are all drawn into grocery stores by promises of unrepeatable price cuts, price match pledges, special promotions and coupons galore. If you use the promotions properly, you can save an enormous amount on your grocery bill. But remember the promotions can either be a menace or a real boon to your grocery budget. Take advantage when you need them and focus on things that will not go off and that you would buy in any case. When you see these offers, get as many as you can afford and store them.

Yellow Tickets

You know what these are: the items are close to their sell-by dates and, in a desperate attempt to prevent them from having to be thrown out, the grocery store will slash the price. But when is the best time to find these deals? Although there are different policies, there are some patterns. The first yellow stickers start appearing by mid-morning, but the mad reductions begin at around seven in the evening. This is when the price can be slashed by three quarters or more. The store will be virtually giving the food away.

Spotting the Yellow Tickets

Most of the store staff will have the authority to reduce prices, but it is at their discretion. Watch out for an employee carefully looking through the stock. If you find something yourself, it can often pay to ask for a reduction. Do not demand it; politeness often gets you a long way. Reduced items that are part of multi-buy offers will give you an even better saving. The till will often deduct the full price discount even though the items have been reduced. This means that on a buy-two-get-one-free offer, with the items reduced to half price, the till might deduct the full price of your free item.

Buy One, Get One Free

A few words of caution, because these buy-one-get-one-free (often known as 'BOGOF' or 'BOGO'), or the similar buy-two-get-one-free deals seem so tempting that it is impossible to believe it is not a bargain:

 Check the competitor stores: Just because they are buy-one-get-one-free, it does not mean they are necessarily cheaper than elsewhere.

 Check alternative products: There is no guarantee that you are getting a bargain.

 Combine savings: If you can use a coupon in conjunction with one of these promotions, then real savings can be made.

 Do you like the product?: If you have not tried this brand before, how will you feel if you have a cupboard full of products you hate?

Would you buy it anyway?: Do not be tempted into buying something you would not normally buy just because there is a promotion.

BOGOF Tactics

Originally, buy-one-get-one-frees were used to get rid of end of season stocks or overstocks. Now they are just a regular marketing tool. The stores price them so that the cost of the item you are paying for is slightly higher than you would normally expect. So watch out, because BOGOFs do not mean you are actually getting both of them at half price. Nevertheless, they can offer real savings.

Making BOGOFs Work For You

So the deal is 'buy two, get one free' (or 'three for two'). But you only need two. Why not trade your extra item with friends and family? They have probably found a similar deal on something else that they can exchange for your extra item. If they regularly shop at one store and you regularly shop at another, you could even find that you have weekly BOGOFs to exchange.

Why BOGOF?

The stores know that 25 per cent of all shoppers buy items just because they are part of a multi-buy deal. And over 80 per cent of all of the promotional activity in the stores are three-for-twos. Most of them are funded by the manufacturer on the basis that the stores can sell more of their mayonnaise or cornflakes. It is the manufacturers who bear the cost of the get-one-free element of the offer, not the store.

Coupon Madness

We have already seen how common coupons can be. But when are the stores desperate enough to up their production of coupons to tempt you in? Research has shown that the summer months are the slowest for coupons and the number of coupons doubles in November and December. Summer coupons tend to focus on outdoor foods to tempt us into barbecuing. By the autumn, canned foods become the focus to convince us that we need to console ourselves over the fall in temperatures with hot soups. By the run-up to Christmas, there is a host of coupons on spices, chocolate and bakery items. In the spring, it is cleaning products and last season's stored fruit and vegetables, like potatoes and apples.

Final Thoughts on Coupons

Some things to watch out for:

 Not necessarily the best deal: If something is on sale without a coupon, it is usually cheaper than the regular price with a coupon.

 Avoid involuntary bulk buying: Always buy the smallest quantity that the coupon allows.

 Keep eyes peeled: Check store entrances and flyers for last-minute coupons.

 Don't be led astray: Only ever use coupons for items you would normally buy anyway.

 Trial purchases: If you want to try something new, wait for the coupons, so that it will not be such a waste of money if you do not like the product.

 Double savings: *If possible*, always use store coupons and manufacturers' coupons together for the same item, making a double saving.

What to Buy

Everyone has their own personal preferences about food. But we will now look at some simple, cheap and easy food to handle and what you should really have in your store cupboard or fridge. First, some key points: if you are buying anything fresh or with a short sell-by date, make sure you are going to eat it that day or the next day, or you will only end up throwing it out; if you are buying dry or store cupboard items, stock up when they are on offer.

The Main Players

Everyone slips into an eating routine. Some of us like pasta; others will prefer to have potatoes or rice with every meal. Some of us will not consider it a meal unless there is meat on the plate. The key to shopping on a budget is to be flexible. The same goes for vegetables; buy what is in season and what is plentiful and that guarantees that you will pay less.

Meat and Poultry

For most portions of meat, you need to be thinking about 100–175 g/4–6 oz per person. Food like beef steak, chicken and roast pork should be around 175–225 g/6–8 oz per person. Do not worry too much about the size of a joint of meat: you can always slice it up and use it for another meal the next day. You can also freeze sliced meat wrapped in kitchen foil in portions. Meat varies in price – consider stewing steak rather than beef steak or other less expensive cuts that can provide you with an equally delicious meal at a fraction of the price, and do not forget minced/ground meat. See the Basic Techniques section (pages 130–153) for more in-depth advice on the different meats and meat cuts that you can cook.

Fish

Oily fish like trout, mackerel and herring are great substitutes for a meat meal. One or two of these whole fish is ideal per person. They are relatively cheap and nutritious too. White fish is getting more expensive, but there are still bargains to be found. A 175–225 g/6–8 oz fillet is more than enough for one person. You can poach, fry or bake white fish. It is simple and is full of nutrition. There are plenty of other options, and do not disregard what you might think are more expensive alternatives. Check out the fresh fish section in your store. They will have promotional offers and they are bound to have reduced items towards the end of the day.

Pasta, Noodles and Rice

As we will see, these can form the basis of any meal. A generous 75 g/3 oz portion per person is ideal. Pasta, noodles and rice are filling and can be combined with vegetables, fish and meat or even just a simple sauce. A large, family-sized bag will provide plenty of meals for a couple and it keeps for ages in the cupboard. Just take out what you need per meal and seal the bag again. You can seal the bag with a washing peg if it is not a self-seal bag.

Vegetables

Eating fresh vegetables is an essential part of a balanced diet. They can be eaten as part of a meal or even as a meal in themselves. Vegetables are very versatile but you must not overcook them or you will lose most of the goodness and flavour.

- **Cost of frozen**: Do not forget that, although frozen vegetables are more convenient and often cheaper, they can be more expensive than fresh *seasonal* vegetables.

- **Variety**: Be flexible with your choice of vegetables.

- **Seasonal**: Buy according to the seasons and keep a look out for special offers.

Freezing Perishable Foods

Most of these perishable items can be frozen. Here is the essential list. Remember they are perishable, so will have a use-by date:

 Bacon: Invaluable chopped up and used in a whole host of pasta and rice dishes. Just freeze in usable portions.

 Vegetables: If you over-buy when they are on offer, you can always prepare them and freeze them. We will look at this way of preserving food a little later.

 Bread: If you are likely to waste bread, then freeze the loaf ready sliced and take slices out as you need them – you can toast them straight from the freezer. However, if you need to defrost them, you may need to plan ahead to give them time to defrost naturally. Bread defrosted in the microwave can turn out soggy!

Multipurpose Essentials

Basic grocery items can allow you to bring together a simple meal. These multipurpose ingredients do not include fresh items but are store-cupboard staples. Try to make sure you always have as many of these items in your store cupboard as possible. They are a worthwhile investment since they are versatile enough for you to be able to use them in a number of different recipes and they do not need replacing every week because they have a really long shelf life.

Condiments, Oils and Sauces

You need to make sure that these items are always available to you because they can be used for so many different things:

 Vegetable oil: For frying and roasting.

 Olive oil: Go for extra virgin olive oil or regular olive oil. They are great for salad dressings and cooking. Since the former is more expensive, you may wish to save it for salad dressings where its flavour will be more appreciated.

Mustard: A universal addition to a cooked dinner or a sandwich.

Ketchup: Great for adding to sauces and pies, as well as its traditional use with chips or fries.

Soy sauce: Adds a good salty flavour and great for stir-fries.

Tomato puree: Essential for pizzas, pasta and lasagne.

Dried Ingredients

In addition to your oils and sauces, your store cupboard should always have:

Rice: Cheap and basic. Go for brown rice; it has a better flavour and is better for you, although it does take longer to cook.

Dried pasta: Quick and easy meals can be made by combining this with a basic tomato sauce and cheese. Go for spaghetti and penne because they are the most versatile. Again, the brown variety is more wholesome but takes a little longer to cook.

Salt: Absolutely essential, but do not over-use it in your cooking.

Pepper: Go for peppercorns (that you use in a grinder) because the flavour is more intense.

Spices: The most essential are curry powder, mixed spice, dried chilli and turmeric. These will allow you to make a host of different recipes.

Dried mixed herbs: Great for sauces, adding flavour to meat dishes and also giving vegetables a boost.

The Vegetable Rack

Again, these are perishable items, but these are the three real staples:

 Potatoes: You can mash them, bake them, chip them or roast them. They are cheap, nutritious and delicious.

 Onions: An extremely versatile vegetable that can add flavour and texture to your meals and stretch the portions. It is a required ingredient in a great many recipes.

 Garlic: Can bring a recipe to life, from pasta sauces to roast vegetables and in marinades.

In the Fridge

These items do have a sell-by date, but they are absolute essentials:

 Butter or margarine: Butter is probably more versatile because you can add it to sauces.

 Cheese: Go for a strong cheddar, as this can be used in a huge variety of dishes.

Eggs: A great stand-by meal with bread or toast and also used in many recipes.

Milk: Not only essential for cereal and hot drinks, but a useful addition to scrambled eggs and a host of other quick meals. Keep some reserves in the freezer.

More Store-cupboard Gems

Now we have looked at the most useful multipurpose ingredients, we can turn our attention to other store cupboard essentials, which you should not be without. Most of them have got long, or almost indefinite, sell-by dates. But you need to regularly check that you have enough of them. Take the advantage of stocking up when they are on special offer, as they will get used if you store them correctly. None of these items will ever be wasted if you manage your store cupboard properly.

Non-perishable Essentials

Here are some more ingredients that you should really keep in your store cupboard:

 Stock cubes: Beef, chicken and vegetable stock in the form of soluble cubes. However, using these all the time instead of making stock fom scratch may not always save you money – the same goes for gravy (see below).

 Gravy powder or granules: Yes, a cheat perhaps, but these are a much quicker and easier alternative to making your own gravy.

Cornflour: For thickening sauces and gravy.

Flour: For home baking and pies, even pasta-making.

Dried milk: A useful standby and also used for baking, bread-making and sauces.

Vinegar: Used in dressings and sauces and some types are used for preserving food.

Essential Cans

Canned food is usually cheaper, quicker and easier and, what is more, many of these canned foods are often on promotion:

- chopped or peeled tomatoes
- baked beans
- kidney beans
- chickpeas
- butterbeans, and many other beans
- sweetcorn
- soups
- tuna fish

- sardines
- corned beef
- frankfurter sausages
- minced beef
- stewed steak
- evaporated milk
- spaghetti in sauce
- other canned vegetables

Essential Desserts

These canned or non-perishable items will give you a quick dessert: blancmange powder, jellies, rice pudding and canned fruit. You can combine evaporated milk and canned fruit for a cheap, tasty and easy dessert if you have unexpected guests. Children love blancmange and it is easy to make with a pint of hot milk and sugar.

Useful Ethnic Ingredients

Every country or region of the world has its own distinctive secret ingredient that brings you a taste of their cuisine. Stocking your kitchen with a handful of these special ingredients can really perk up your food and give you a taste of the exotic. Though they may seem expensive, they are a worthwhile investment as they are long lasting and can be added to a variety of dishes, from simple pastas and stews to marinades for meat. Invaluable examples include:

- Thai fish sauce
- Mexican or North African chilli sauce (or Thai sweet chilli sauce)
- Chinese or Japanese rice vinegar and soy sauce
- Italian balsamic vinegar and wine vinegars from all over the world

What Kinds of Foods are Cheapest?

The doom-mongers are warning us that the age of cheap food is at an end because of shortages across the world. Even staples like rice are increasing in price. As the world competes for food supplies, coupled with poor harvests, bread, pasta and eggs are on the rise too. Every time the oil prices rise, up goes the price of food. But there are still bargains to be had if you shop smart and stick to your budget.

Make Your Own Meals

It is tempting, isn't it, a ready-made meal? Five minutes in the microwave and it is done. But it is processed food, with poor-quality ingredients. It is packed with additives to cover up the poor quality and taste. Cheese spread and slices are just as bad. You do not have to be a gourmet cook to make your own meals. With planning, good ingredients and a well-stocked fridge, freezer and cupboard, you can do it. The recipes at the end of the book will give you some good ideas for soups and starters, fish and seafood, meat and poultry, vegetables and desserts and sweet treats.

What About Going Veggie?

Some people have realized that beans, lentils and pulses are not only an excellent source of protein, but far cheaper than meat and fish. As an alternative, you can make the meat go even further by mixing in beans, lentils, chickpeas or even baked beans. You do not have to be a vegetarian to take advantage of these price and health benefits. Why not decide that at least one of your weekly menus will be a vegetarian one?

Fresh Seasonal Food

Shoppers can buy strawberries all year round, buy turkeys every day and enjoy the most exotic fruit and vegetables, but at a price! Somewhere in the world, these foods are in season. They are shipped halfway across the planet to the grocery stores. They are premium priced. However, many of these have their own natural seasons in your country and this is when they are at their cheapest and most plentiful. There is no substitute in terms of price or nutritional value. The market is glutted with them at certain times of the year, so stock up when they are cheap. Freeze or preserve them and enjoy them all year round.

Food that Will Not Last

As we have discussed, food can be marked down when it is approaching its sell-by date. The different dates on packaging can be confusing, however, so it is worth clarifying what these different dates mean:

- ✅ **'Display until' or 'sell by'**: These are instructions to the store, telling them when to take them off the shelves. More relevant to you are the use-by and best-before dates.

- ✅ **'Use by'**: If an item is past this date, it is probably best to throw it away. Do not take a risk with meat, fish or eggs.

- ✅ **'Best before'**: This usually appears on longer-lasting products. It is usually safe to eat but it will not be at its best quality past this date.

Canned Food

Before nearly every household had a freezer, canning was the way to preserve foods. They still provide excellent value for money. You will still benefit from buying canned food in season, as the stores are likely to run special offers because the supplies are so plentiful. The great thing about canned food is that you can store them for months. Look out for damaged cans though: they may be reduced in price, but you cannot guarantee that they will last quite as long, as air may have got into the can.

Dried and Packaged Foods

Dried, freeze-dried and dehydrated foods can be a great emergency supply. You can buy all sorts of items, including dried vegetables, dehydrated eggs and dry mixes such as pudding and bread mix. Freeze-dried and dehydrated foods can be bought online from specific websites such as www.survivalacres.com in the US – aside from the benefits of long life, easy storage and low cost, it is claimed that treating foods in this way loses fewer nutrients than freezing or canning. According to the aforementioned website, because many of these foods are packaged in an oxygen-free environment, there is no need for additives or preservatives to keep the food fresh.

Nutritional Facts

When you plan your menus and your shopping lists, you need to have a basic understanding of nutrition. Our bodies need a variety of different foods in order for them to work properly and for us to remain healthy. Food on a budget does not mean that nutritious food and well-balanced meals are off the agenda. Food should have flavour and look great, but it should be good for us too.

What are Nutrients?

These are chemical compounds that are present in food. They supply energy for the body and help build and replace cells. They also help to regulate our bodies' processes. Not including water, there are five categories of nutrients: carbohydrates, fats, proteins, vitamins and minerals. To this list, you could also add 'fibre'. This is not really a nutrient as such, but is nevertheless very necessary for a healthy, functioning body.

What About Calories?

A calorie (written as 'kcal' on food labels, as a food 'calorie' is in fact a 'kilocalorie') is just a measurement of energy. It is defined as the amount of heat needed to raise the temperature of 1 kg of water by 1°C. We need this energy, but there is enormous debate about how many calories adult humans need to eat every day in order to remain healthy. Broadly, men need around 2,700 calories a day and women about 2,000. Up to 60 per cent of those calories can come from carbohydrates, 20 per cent from proteins and up to 20 per cent from fats. Expectant mothers need to take in more per day and if you are breast-feeding, you need at least another 500 calories.

Calorie Content in Carbohydrate, Protein and Fat

Without sufficient food energy, a body cannot function properly. So how many calories can the three basic nutritional elements give you?

- **Carbohydrate**: 28 g/1 oz of carbohydrate contains 112 calories.

- **Protein**: The same amount of protein contains 112 calories.

- **Fat**: The same amount of fat contains 252 calories.

Food from animals tends to be higher in fat, and some products, such as fruit, vegetables and grains, are naturally low in fat. But beware because some grocery items like French fries or croissants are prepared with fat.

Carbohydrates

These are an important source of food energy. Carbohydrates exist in two forms: complex and simple. Complex carbohydrates, which contain starches and fibre, are the best as they provide a slower-burning and thus more constant supply of energy. Complex carbohydrates that contain refined starches are not so good for you, however. Simple carbohydrates are sugars. Some are natural whilst others are refined – again, the refined kind are particularly bad for you. Examples of foods that contain carbohydrates are:

Complex carbohydrates (starches): Brown rice; wholemeal breads, grains, cereals, flour and pasta; beans and peas; root vegetables; bananas.

 Complex carbohydrates (refined starches): White bread, flour, pasta and rice; processed breakfast cereals; pizzas; biscuits, pastries and cakes.

 Simple carbohydrates (sugars): The natural ones are in fruit and vegetables. Even these can cause tooth decay.

 Simple carbohydrates (refined sugars): Chocolate; honey; jams; soft drinks; sweets and snacks; prepared food and sauces; biscuits, cakes and pastries.

Fibre

Fibre is basically carbohydrate that the body cannot use, so it does not supply the body with energy. However, it is essential in helping the intestinal tract to work properly and flush out waste. Dietary fibre can also prevent some kinds of cancer. It can be found in whole grains and fruit and vegetables, provided they are eaten raw.

Fats

Cholesterol (an element of animal fat) is often portrayed as the developed world's health time bomb. It is linked to heart disease and it is found in a wide variety of food, such as beef, pork, poultry, butter, egg yolks, liver and dairy products. However, cholesterol is an important part of a healthy body and it is only when it reaches high levels in the blood that it becomes a danger. In fact, fat in general is a very necessary element of the diet, but some are better than others:

Saturated fats: These are fats that are solid at room temperature. You find them in dairy products, animal fats, fatty meat, some oils and foods such as chocolate. These are the ones that contribute to health problems.

 Polyunsaturated fats: Found in fish and soya beans, sunflower and corn oils. They are considered to be more healthy options.

Monounsaturated fats: These can be found in olive oil and whole grains and nuts. These too are considered to be more healthy.

Trans fat: This is a type of unsaturated fat that can be polyunsaturated or monounsaturated, but which has become more like a saturated fat, usually by virtue of a process of partial hydrogenation. Trans fats have been linked to an elevated risk of coronary heart disease, so it is advisable to avoid foods (typically processed foods) which contain partially hydrogenated vegetable oils.

Proteins

Proteins are amino acids, necessary for all sorts of complicated functions within our cells. The body can make its own amino acids, but there are eight types that it cannot make, so we need to get them from food. This is why we need to have dairy products, poultry, fish, eggs and meat in our diet. You can get all the amino acids you need if you eat beans and rice together, or if you combine cornmeal bread and chilli beans. Proteins are essential for building body tissue and the body can also use them for energy.

Vitamins and Minerals

Both of these are essential, but neither contains energy. Key vitamins and minerals, and examples of which foods contain them, are as follows:

- **Vitamin A**: Contained in mangos, broccoli, squashes, carrots and pumpkins.

- **Vitamin B**: Contained in spinach, peas, tomatoes, watermelons and potatoes.

- **Vitamin C**: Contained in spinach, peppers, kiwi fruits, strawberries and citrus fruits.

- **Vitamin D**: Contained in egg yolks, liver and fatty fish.

- **Vitamin E**: Contained in wheat germ, avocados, sweet potatoes and tofu.

- **Vitamin K**: Contained in leafy green vegetables, broccoli, cabbage and liver.

- **Calcium**: A mineral contained in milk, cheese and sardines.

- **Iron**: A mineral contained in artichokes, spinach and clams.

- **Iodine**: A mineral contained in salt, seafood, bread and milk.

- **Sodium**: The easiest way to take in the mineral sodium is through salt, but not too much because it causes high blood pressure. It is also in soy sauce, bread and milk.

- **Potassium**: A mineral contained in potatoes, green beans and bananas.

The Balanced Diet

You do not need to know the science behind nutrition, nor to make things complicated for yourself. Simply aim for a truly balanced diet and your body should receive everything it needs. Follow some golden rules:

 Variety: Eat a variety of foods to provide your body with everything it needs. 'Eat a rainbow a day to keep the doctor away.'

 Exercise: Balance your food with physical activity, to improve fitness and help your body make the most of its healthy diet.

 Natural and wholesome: Eat plenty of whole grains, vegetables and fruit.

Keep a check on fats: Avoid saturated fats to keep your cholesterol down.

Keep a check on sugars: Do not include too many sugars in your diet.

Keep a check on salt: Reduce the amount of salt and sodium to avoid high blood pressure – adults should consume no more than 6 g a day.

 Drink alcohol in moderation: It supplies calories but little or no nutrients.

Grow Your Own

The nutritional rewards and sense of achievement in growing your own food just cannot be compared. Even if you are short on space and do not even have a garden, it is not impossible. The thrill of harvesting your own food is incomparable. Of course, it is going to take work and you do need some essential items initially. But it is nowhere near as difficult as you would imagine. Look forward to that magic moment when your own fruit and vegetables are ready to eat.

Growing Your Own Vegetables

Like all plants, vegetables are going to need soil, nutrients, water and sunlight. But they can be grown as easily on a small patio or beside your back door, or even on a windowsill. Some people even grow them completely indoors beside a sunny window. You can grow vegetables all year round using rotation, switching the type of vegetables you are growing to suit the seasons. The added bonus is that you are not only going to be able to eat the vegetables, but the plants themselves are a really attractive addition to your patio whilst they are growing.

Choosing the Right Kind of Vegetables

Do not worry if you do not have an enormous amount of space. A window box can supply you with enough salad to last you through the summer. Plenty of vegetables can be grown in pots, and potatoes can be grown in bags or in a stack of tyres or a dustbin. Think organic – you will not need to spend on fertilizers or growth enhancers and you are unlikely to need insecticides. Your choice of vegetables includes:

- cress
- tomatoes
- salad leaves
- potatoes
- beans and peas
- cabbage
- carrots
- courgettes/zucchini
- broccoli

Pots

Here are some examples of how you can grow your own fruit and vegetables with very little space, time or effort:

Tomatoes: All they need is a generous pot space. Water them daily and feed them about once a week with a regularly available proprietary tomato food. Nip out the side shoots to encourage them to fruit.

Salad leaves: Lambs lettuce, rocket or quick-growing radishes are all ideal. You can get salad all summer from a handful of plants. Sow them from seed at two-week intervals for a continuous supply.

Strawberries: They could not be easier to grow in a pot or in a window box. They like rich soil and you must not allow them to dry out. Watch the white flowers turn into fruit, but be careful to cover them with some netting so the birds don't eat them first!

Carrier bags

Potatoes are the ideal candidates for carrier-bag cultivation. Notice how your store-bought potatoes begin to sprout after a week or so? Carefully select the ones with the healthiest looking sprouts and place them in an egg carton on the windowsill. When the sprouts are

strong and the chance of a frost has passed, get three store carrier bags and place them one inside another. Fill with compost and plant your sprouting potatoes about 10 cm/4 in deep. Hang them from a hook by the back door but do not forget to water them regularly – without over-watering. When you have strong plants, you should have small potatoes. When the plants flower, your potatoes should be ready to eat. Slice the carrier bags open and harvest.

Freezing Your Crop

Freezing your crop means you need not worry about bumper harvests going to waste. If you have not got a freezer, there are plenty of second-hand ones available. Ninety per cent of freezers are dumped when they are actually still in good working order. They may just not be the latest model.

Most vegetables need to be blanched before freezing. This means you need to immerse them in boiling water. The blanching destroys enzymes that affect the flavour, colour and texture. When you prepare your vegetables for blanching, you need to trim off outer leaves, wash them thoroughly and you can even cut and prepare them as if you were going to cook them straight away. So if you like batons, slices, diced or whole, they will be ready in the freezer when you want to eat them. Once you have blanched your vegetables, let them cool, then put them in freezer bags in portions. If your freezer has a super or fast setting, this is ideal. The quicker the food freezes, the more goodness is retained. Blanching times vary, but here are some guidelines (*see also* page 111 for more discussion of preparing vegetables for the freezer):

- courgettes – 1 minute
- beans – 3 minutes
- squashes – 3 minutes
- carrots – 2 to 5 minutes

Growing Your Own Herbs

Growing your own herbs provides you not only with delicious ingredients for recipes and tasty surprises for your salads, but also wonderful colours and aromas that you can enjoy all year round. There is no comparison with freshly picked herbs that you have grown for yourself; dried herbs come nowhere near. Most of the herbs love warm, sunny spots, so windowsills and window boxes are ideal. This helps them develop their distinctive aromas and it makes your kitchen smell fresh too.

Ideal Herbs

There is a wonderful variety of herbs that you can grow; the first three in this list are the most hardy and useful. You can either buy them as tiny plants or you can grow them from seed:

 Basil: A wonderful, sweet aniseed flavour, great with baked tomatoes or buttered carrots.

Chives: These have a fantastic onion flavour and they have got pretty, lilac pink flowers.

 Mint: This will grow and grow, so make sure you do not let it get too big. It is fantastic with potatoes and you can make your own mint sauce. Try freezing it in ice cube trays so you have always got some.

Parsley: Cut off any flowers that form and you can harvest all year round. Each plant should last for at least two years.

Rosemary: This is an evergreen plant that gives you a warm, savoury flavour and is fantastic in stuffings and with lamb.

Sage: An aromatic evergreen bush. It has pretty leaves and you can buy a purple variety. Both types are great with meat.

Thyme: Delicious savoury, aromatic leaves. Can be gathered all year round. Try lemon thyme for a really strong flavour.

Drying and Freezing Your Herbs

Herbs have maximum flavour just before they flower. So cut and dry them, put the shoots in a brown paper bag and store them. Crush them when they are dry and put them in airtight containers. This will retain their flavour. Some herbs lose their flavour when they are dried, but you can freeze these. Put sprigs of mint and parsley into an ice cube tray, or put sprigs of herbs into plastic bags, and freeze them. They will not keep their shape, but they will keep most of their flavour.

Indoors or Outdoors?

Window Boxes

Depth can be an issue, so avoid planting root vegetables in window boxes, as they will not thrive. Why not combine growing your own food with a wonderful display by mixing in herbs and salad leaves? It will give you year-round colour and, if the frost is too keen, then bring the window box indoors to protect the leaves at night. If you have got a flat roof, then why not turn it into a garden? Do not overburden it, but you can easily lie out grow bags, pots and wooden boxes to turn that wasted space into a market garden!

Indoors

Most of the herbs will flourish indoors, as long as they have got sufficient sunlight. On warm days, put them on the windowsill anyway. Some of the vegetables will flourish indoors, like tomato plants and strawberry plants. But do not forget, they want sunlight too, and they need to be regularly watered and occasionally fed. A lot of the root vegetables simply need too much space and soil depth but peppers and even miniature fruit trees will happily go about their business in your hallway or living room. Do not forget that central heating will dry out their soil more quickly, so keep them well watered.

Kitchen Basics

PACKED WITH •MONEY SAVING• IDEAS & TIPS

Cleanliness

Cooking can be messy and it is important to make sure that your kitchen is always clean and hygienic. Various nasty bugs, in the form of bacteria and viruses, can thrive in an unclean kitchen or even in a clean one when nooks and crannies have been ignored. Famous brand names would have us believe that they have a solution for every cleaning and hygiene worry. They also aim to convince us that they are formulated especially and hundreds of scientists have spent decades developing the products. This could not be further from the truth!

Cheapest Cleaning Products

Even the branded cleaners basically consist of one or two active ingredients. Once we know what they are, it is far cheaper to buy them in bulk and just simply dilute them. Many of the cheaper cleaners actually work even better than some of the big names. However, a word of advice: it is dangerous to mix some chemicals. If you were to mix ammonia with chlorine bleach, the gas that would be created could be fatal.

Branded

Huge multinational companies, like Proctor & Gamble, Unilever and SC Johnson, produce a bewildering range of cleaning products. They are all backed up with tested claims and they have enormous marketing budgets to persuade us that their creams, sprays and liquids do a far better job than anything else on the market. They might do, but at a price – and you do not always have to pay that high price. However, we should not disregard these branded products, especially if they are on special offer or are part of a multi-buy deal. But bear in mind that own-label, multipurpose and home-made cleaning products will probably do just as good a job.

When to Buy Branded

Like all of the other products in the grocery store, branded cleaning products are often offered as part of a special deal. The manufacturers may provide the grocery store with the free item in the buy-one-get-one-free deal, with the purpose of convincing you to switch your brand, having first tempted you to try it. Play the game and switch brands, but when a competing brand has a similar deal the following month you can switch to them. Switching makes sense and saves you money.

Own Brand

Just like any other product, an own-label cleaner is often made in exactly the same factory, in exactly the same conditions, with precisely the same formula as the branded product. There might be slightly weaker bleach, it may smell of pine instead of lemon or it might be less gritty and abrasive. Own brand does not necessarily mean watered down or less effective. In fact, in many tests, the own-brand products are superior to the branded ones, or at least as good.

Value Cleaning Products

Value cleaning products, or unknown or unnamed, are pretty much at the lowest end in terms of price. These are perfectly safe, usable and effective. But do not expect a premium quality product. The cheapest possible ingredients will be used. The likelihood is that if you find something that works well for you, you might not be able to find it again. Therein lies the problem: if it is cheap, do you stock up and take the risk that it will work, or do you try it out, discover that it is great and then never see it again? Many discount stores have their own regular, value brands. Some of the unknown brands are in fact well known in other countries. It is probably worth giving them a try.

Multipurpose

How many households have got a cupboard full of cleaning products, each with their own specific job? A hob cleaner, stainless steel shiner, bleaches, anti-bacterial sprays, and the list goes on. To cut down on space, time and money, consider some of the multipurpose cleaners. A spray that cleans, degreases, shines and is anti-bacterial should sort out nearly all of your work surfaces and your kitchen hygiene issues. The problem is that these are often branded products, so they are premium priced. Watch out for new promotions, particularly when a new brand is launched on to the market.

Natural and Eco-friendly

We should all quite rightly be concerned with the planet and the effect of pouring buckets of bleach down our sinks and toilets. There is a growing trend towards buying natural, eco-friendly cleaning products. But are they not just branded products with a different set of features to attract us? Natural products have also found their way into own-brand product lines. Playing on our concerns, the stores will always add a little to the price of these eco-friendly products, knowing that we are prepared to pay slightly more and shaming us into doing it.

Ingredients for Home-made Cleaning

We really cannot over-stress the importance of being careful in making your own cleaning products. If you are ever in doubt about mixing two chemicals together, then do not do it. Most of the home-made cleaning solutions only need one or two fairly harmless additives. It is always a wise precaution to use gloves anyway when you are cleaning. You do not quite know how your skin might react to neat ingredients. Do not assume that because you have never had a reaction before that you will not have one now. You can become allergic to anything at any time.

White Vinegar

This can dissolve dirt, limescale and soap scum. It can also act as a natural deodorizer, as it absorbs odours and does not just cover them up. It is also a great fabric softener because it cuts down detergent residue. You can use equal proportions of white vinegar and water to clean your worktop surfaces. Stubborn stains can be removed if you heat the vinegar up then leave it on for 15 minutes. Using it neat can take away those hard water limescale deposits. It can also cut straight through soap scum. You can use undiluted white vinegar to clean your enamel, so it is great for ceramic tiles, cooker hoods and tops and kitchen sinks. Work it into your tap head to remove limescale build up.

Bicarbonate of Soda (AKA Baking Soda)

This is a great alternative to scouring powders. Sprinkle it on to a damp sponge and wipe away grimy deposits. You can make a paste if you mix it with water. Apply it to the surface and leave it for 20 minutes. It can also help unclog blocked drains: pour it down the drain with a small amount of hot water, leave it overnight, then flush it out.

Rubbing Alcohol

This is also known as isopropyl alcohol. It is great for cleaning glass, mirrors, chrome and ceramic tiles. To make your own multipurpose cleaning product, mix equal amounts of the rubbing alcohol with water and white vinegar. This will give you a great all-round cleaner that can be used on most surfaces. Go for 70-per-cent rubbing alcohol. The 90-per-cent solution evaporates very quickly, but it will leave you with a smear-free finish.

Ammonia

This is brilliant for cleaning windows and work surfaces. Mix equal amounts of rubbing alcohol and water (250 ml/8 fl oz/1 cup each) with 1 tablespoon household ammonia. This makes a fantastic glass cleaner. To make an all-purpose cleaner, add 1 teaspoon ammonia and 1 teaspoon laundry detergent to 500 ml/18 fl oz/2 cups water. Mix it in an empty spray bottle to make a handy dispenser. This solution can deal with nearly all of your cleaning needs in the kitchen.

Lemon Juice

Lemon juice is ideal to dissolve dirt and get rid of smudges on work surfaces. If you mix 250 ml/8 fl oz/1 cup olive oil with 125 ml/4 fl oz/½ cup lemon juice, you can make a brilliant furniture polish. Make sure that you mix it well. Apply the solution to a clean cloth, spread the mixture evenly over the surface, then turn the cloth over to polish off.

Borax and Cornflour

Borax, or sodium borate, is a brilliant alternative to bleach and ammonia. It is a natural product that kills mould, mildew and bacteria. It also has the advantage of deodorizing, removing stains and boosting the power of any soap you may be using. Be careful because borax can be toxic to children and pets. Cornflour/cornstarch is also a useful natural cleaning product because it absorbs oil and grease.

Herbs, Essential Oils and Toothpaste

If you are growing your own herbs on the windowsill, why not put them to another great value use? The aromatic herbs will give you a wonderfully natural disinfecting agent and a fragrance. The same can be said for essential oils, although of course these can be far more expensive. We will be talking about other ways to make use of worn out toothbrushes later, but toothpaste itself is a great mild abrasive. Put some on an old toothbrush and use it to clean off grease and stains around your taps.

Washing Soda

This is also known as sodium carbonate. You can use it to clean clothes and to soften water. It is also great at cutting through grease and disinfecting. If you use it with soap, it will increase the cleaning power.

Simple Cleaning Solutions

Here are some great recipes to make your own cleaning products for the kitchen. They all use natural ingredients, such as vinegar, lemon juice and baking soda. The majority of them are non-toxic and environmentally safe, but always be careful. The added bonus is that they are really inexpensive.

Handy Hints

To save yourself time and money, make your cleaners in advance and always try to buy the ingredients in bulk. You can always make large batches and store them in airtight plastic containers or spray bottles. Make sure you label all your ingredients and keep them out of reach of children and pets. Most of these cleaners are not poisonous, but they could be dangerous if swallowed. You can always add your favourite essential oils or herbs to any of these solutions to give you more fragrance.

Air Fresheners and Deodorizers

✔ **Fragrant spray**: Cloves, cinnamon sticks and allspice simmered in a pot of water for 1 to 2 hours will give you a great 'essential oil' that will freshen and deodorize the air. You can use orange or lemon rind if you prefer.

✅ **Bicarbonate of soda spray**: Dissolve a small amount of bicarb/baking soda in 475 ml/16 fl oz/2 cups hot water and add the juice of 1 lemon; pour the contents into a spray bottle when it has cooled. This will produce a more deodorizing spray than using fragrance alone.

✅ **Absorbing and neutralizing odours**: Other ways to deodorize include placing 2–3 slices of white bread into your refrigerator; placing an open container of bicarbonate of soda in your fridge or cupboard; or leaving some vinegar or charcoal in a bowl.

All-purpose Cleaners

We have already seen that vinegar is a good surface cleaner, but if you mix it with salt it is even better. Other great all-purpose cleaners include:

✅ **Soda paste**: For a basic 'cream cleaner', dissolve 4 tablespoons bicarbonate of soda into 900 ml/1½ pts/1 qt warm water.

✅ **Soapy solution**: Mix 3 tablespoons vinegar, half a teaspoon washing soda and half a teaspoon liquid soap with 500 ml/18 fl oz/2 cups hot water.

Borax the Disinfectant

Cleaning with ordinary soap and hot water will kill some bacteria. But borax is a cheap solution. Here are some ways to use it:

✅ **Strong solution**: Mix 100 g/4 oz/ ½ cup borax into 4.5 l/8 pts/4½ qts hot water or undiluted white vinegar.

> **Fragrance**: If you want to add a few sprigs of thyme, rosemary or lavender, let them steep for 10 minutes.

> **Gentler solution**: As an alternative, you could mix the juice of a lemon, 475 ml/16 fl oz/2 cups hot water and 2 tablespoons borax to make an all-purpose disinfectant.

Glass Cleaners

Undiluted vinegar or equal parts vinegar and water, or even the juice of half a lemon and 475 ml/16 fl oz/2 cups water, will give you a good glass cleaner. For a no-streaks glass cleaner, mix 50 ml/2 fl oz/$\frac{1}{4}$ cup white vinegar, 1 tablespoon cornflour/cornstarch and 900 ml/$1\frac{1}{2}$ pts/1 qt warm water. Apply this mixture to the glass with a sponge or use a spray bottle. Wipe dry with crumpled up newspaper and buff it to a shine with a dry cloth.

Scouring Powder

Bicarbonate of soda/baking soda and table salt can be used as mild abrasives. All you need to do is apply them to the surface, scour and then rinse. To make a soft, non-abrasive scourer, mix 50 g/2 oz/$\frac{1}{4}$ cup borax, $\frac{1}{2}$ teaspoon lemon oil and enough liquid soap to create a creamy paste. Put a small amount of the mixture on a sponge. Use it to wash down the surface and then rinse well.

Enamel Cleaner

Bicarbonate of soda/baking soda and white vinegar mixed together will clean and deodorize enamel. If you leave a small amount of ready-mixed borax and lemon juice on stubborn stains for two hours, it should remove the marks. If you have an enamel sink, drop a denture tablet into a full sink of hot water and leave it to soak overnight. You can also mix equal amounts of borax and white vinegar, or even sprinkle some borax into your sink or enamel drainer, then spray on some vinegar. Leave it for an hour or two, or even overnight, and then rinse off.

Drain cleaner

We all have slow drains from time to time and this simple recipe will keep them fresh
and clear:

- 100 g/4 oz/$\frac{1}{2}$ cup bicarbonate of soda/baking soda
- 250 ml/8 fl oz/1 cup white vinegar
- $\frac{1}{2}$ lemon
- 4.5 l/8 pts/$4\frac{1}{2}$ qts boiling water

No need to even mix any of this, just pop the lemon into the boiling water. First, pour the
baking soda down the drain, follow it quickly with the vinegar. Allow this to foam, then flush
the drain out with the boiling water.

Tile Cleaner

You can use bicarbonate of soda/baking soda just as you would use a scouring powder, rubbing
it with a damp sponge. For more stubborn stains, wipe down the tiles with neat vinegar, then
apply the soda. Rub with a sponge. Vinegar does not leave a film on the tiles. Bicarb can
also be used to clean the grout between the tiles: if you mix 600 g/1$\frac{1}{3}$ lb/3 cups soda with
250 ml/8 fl oz/1 cup warm water, this will create a smooth paste. Scrub it into the grout using
an old toothbrush or a sponge and then rinse off.

Rust Stain and Limescale Remover

If you use full-strength vinegar or lemon juice directly on a rust stain, then you have a
good chance of making it disappear. You may need to reapply several times. If you can
immerse the rust stain in the neat vinegar or lemon juice, then it should work much more
quickly. This will also work on stubborn limescale deposits. The major problem is that the
lime deposits often form in difficult areas. Consider suspending a small plastic container
filled with vinegar or lemon juice directly underneath the spout of your tap overnight to
completely clear out the limescale.

Sink and Tap Cleaner

This will work on stainless steel, chrome, ceramics, porcelain, enamel or fibreglass. Wipe a solution of 2 tablespoons bicarb/baking soda and 900 ml/1½ pts/1 qt warm water on to the fixtures and then rinse off. If there are any stubborn lime deposits, then use neat vinegar. Soak some cloths in a small bowl of vinegar for around an hour before you use them. This will clean off the lime and shine up the chrome.

Mildew Remover

Mildew can best be removed by mixing equal amounts of neat vinegar and borax into an equal amount of warm water. Simply apply the solution (wearing gloves) on to the affected area. If you apply this solution from time to time, even if mildew is not visibly present, it will act as a permanent deterrent.

Oven Cleaner

One of the best pieces of advice is prevention. Always put a sheet of kitchen foil at the bottom of your oven, but make sure it is not touching the heating element. You can then clean up spills as soon as they happen. One of the easiest ways to keep your oven clean is to sprinkle some bicarb/baking soda or salt over a spill while the oven is still warm. If the spill is dry, you will need to wet it before you sprinkle on the powder. When the oven is cool, you can scrape the spill off and wash the area clean. You can also clean up using a combination of bicarb, water, liquid soap and salt: sprinkle the water on the oven surface, cover the wet area with bicarb and leave it overnight. The next day, wipe off the soda solution and apply the liquid soap with a scouring pad. Rinse clean. You can also get rid of build-ups of grease by dipping your cleaning cloth in vinegar and water.

Extreme Oven Cleaning

We are not suggesting that you jump out of an aeroplane along with your oven, but this is the most hazardous, last-resort option. Pour 120 ml/4 fl oz/$\frac{1}{2}$ cup household ammonia into a small bowl, place the bowl in the oven, close the door and leave to stand overnight. If surfaces have stubborn stains, use fine steel wool to scrub them, then wash with soapy water and rinse thoroughly. When using the ammonia, make sure you wear gloves and open a window.

Refrigerator and Freezer Cleaner

This will work both on the inside and on the outside of your refrigerator or freezer. Simply dissolve 2 tablespoons bicarbonate of soda/baking soda into 900 ml/1$\frac{1}{2}$ pts/1 qt warm water. Use it to wipe all the surfaces. If you have stubborn marks, make up some bicarb paste with a small amount of water. Make sure that you rinse off with a clean, wet cloth. The shelves and the vegetable bins can easily be washed out with simple hot, soapy water, but make sure that you rinse them well and that they are completely dry before putting them back.

Pots and Pans Cleaner

Is your favourite pot or pan burnt? Does it have cremated food encrusted on the sides? Try this solution: either soak the pan in, or boil in the pan, a solution of 2 tablespoons bicarbonate of soda/baking soda for every 900 ml/1½ pts/1 qt water that the pan will take; let the pan stand until the crust has been loosened and then wash it as normal. You can clean out greasy pans by adding 2 teaspoons bicarb when you wash them normally.

Copper Pans and Nonstick Cookware Cleaner

To clean copper pans, sprinkle coarse salt over the surface and then rub the salt into the stains with half a fresh cut lemon. To deal with stains on nonstick surfaces, simply pour some water into the cookware, then add 2 tablespoons bicarbonate of soda/baking soda. Place the cookware on the hob and heat, allowing it to simmer for 5–10 minutes. Make sure that you do not let the mixture boil. After this, wash the cookware in soapy water, rinse and dry. To keep a good sheen, give it a light coating of cooking oil or olive oil.

Baking Dishes and Other Dishes

Soak enamel, ceramic or glass baking dishes in hot, soapy water. Then sprinkle salt or bicarbonate of soda/baking soda over the stained areas. Leave for 5 minutes and then rinse thoroughly. For other dishes, you can use equal parts borax and washing soda to remove stubborn stains. Alternatively, you could use bicarb and liquid soap made into a paste.

Floor Cleaner

If your floor is not waxed, then you can use a solution of the below ingredients. Mix the ingredients thoroughly and make sure that the washing soda is completely dissolved. Mop the floor as usual and this will remove any greasy spots.

 250 ml/8 fl oz/1 cup vinegar
50 g/2 oz/¼ cup washing soda
1 tbsp liquid soap
9 l/2 gal hot water

General-purpose Metal Cleaners

Different approaches can be taken for each type of metal. Toothpaste is great for cleaning silver, as is a paste made up from bicarbonate of soda/baking soda and water. If your silver is tarnished, soak it in salted water inside an aluminium container, then just wipe clean. For brass, mix equal parts salt and flour with a little white vinegar. For chrome, use undiluted vinegar. Rubbing lemon juice and salt or warmed vinegar and salt is a great way to clean up copper. Stainless steel can be returned to a shine with a paste made up of bicarb and water.

Vinyl Cleaners

Many work surfaces and floors are now made of vinyl, as are some chopping boards. Simply make a solution of 50 g/2 oz/¼ cup washing soda and 250 ml/8 fl oz/1 cup boiling water, making sure the washing soda is fully dissolved, then apply the mixture with a sponge. Wipe down with a damp cloth.

Hygiene

Kitchens are places where microbes, bacteria and viruses can thrive. They can cause food poisoning, but they can easily be spread around the kitchen by your hands, the chopping board, knives, cloths and utensils. If care is not taken, they can cross-contaminate other foods, so good kitchen hygiene is essential. It is important to get into the habit of cleaning as you go. All crockery and utensils need to be washed in hot water with detergent. You must change the water regularly and rinse the items in clean hot water, leaving them to drain until dry.

Chopping Boards

There is a trend towards wooden chopping boards, not just because they look great but because they have tannin in them, which is a natural antibacterial agent. They also do not dull your knives so much. You need to scrub the board after you have used it with hot, soapy water. Rinse and then allow to dry. If you have a plastic board, then you can clean and deodorize it by putting 1 teaspoon bleach into 1l/1³⁄₄ pts/1 qt water. Clean the board and allow it to stand for 5 minutes before you rinse and dry it.

Worktops and Cupboards

Most of our kitchen worktops are laminate. This means that they are very easy to keep hygienic. Wash them down every day with warm, soapy water. Do not forget to get into the nooks and crannies regularly with an old toothbrush when required. Do not use abrasive cleaners like steel wool or anything gritty. This will permanently damage the surface.

Bins

Always put a sack inside your kitchen bin/garbage can. This will not only keep your bin generally cleaner, but it will also mean that it is far easier to deal with the waste. Whatever precautions you take, bins will inevitably begin to smell. Remember the following points:

 Frequency: Empty or take out the bag to the outside bins regularly.

 Wash it: Wash the bin itself in hot soapy water to avoid seepage from the sack smelling. The outside of the bin is just as important as the inside, so wash it too.

 Ban smelly foods: Do not be tempted to put strong smelling foods into the inside bin, but pop them straight in the outside bin.

Organic matter: If you are lucky enough to have a garden, always put vegetable peelings and other uncooked vegetable waste into a compost bin.

✅ **Don't forget the other one**: The recycle bin also needs washing regularly.

Kitchen Cloths

Kitchen cloths and tea towels are a major source of cross-contamination. They need to be changed regularly. It is preferable to use disposable cloths or paper towels. Regularly soak your dishcloths in bleach in order to ensure that all bacteria carried on them are killed off. Don't ever use the same cloth for two different tasks. Never use the same one used for the floor for the chopping board. Never use the same one you use to wipe your bin to wash down your work surfaces.

Hands

Did you know that if you wear a ring there can be literally tens of millions of germs underneath it? They also hide under watches and bracelets. A 1 mm hair follicle can be home to 50,000 germs. Also, a thousand times more germs are spread from damp hands than from dry hands. This does not mean that you do not need to wash your hands regularly. Always wash them before preparing food or eating. Always wash them after you have handled raw food and before touching any other food or kitchen utensils. Meat, fish, poultry and eggs are all potential carriers of germs. The most frequently missed areas when we wash our hands are the fingertips and the gap between the thumb and the rest of the hand.

Equipment

Watch any cookery show on TV and you will see the chefs using a bewildering variety of tools and gadgets to speed up preparation time and cooking of food. There seems to be a pan or utensil for everything from scooping out avocados to picking up an olive from a dish. They are not all essential. Think about our ancestors: they cooked on open fires and probably only had a single pot and a multipurpose knife. You don't have to return to the caves, but you certainly do not have to spend a fortune on kitchen gadgets.

Essential Equipment to Buy

It will always be a matter of argument as to what is necessary and what is not necessary in a kitchen. You could probably get away with not buying some of the equipment we have listed here as being essential. But these are all useful, multipurpose, labour-saving devices that do not cost a fortune.

Cookware

Cookware includes all of your saucepans and frying pans, as well as oven dishes. If you are going to spend money on cookware, then really you need to buy the best that you can afford. The heavier the better; you want smooth bases and tight-fitting lids because this will mean that food will cook more evenly and more quickly than when using the cheaper cookware. You want tough and durable handles and, ideally, all your cookware should be capable of being put into the oven. This means it is even more multipurpose.

Saucepans

A basic saucepan set should ideally consist of a small, medium and large saucepan, plus a lidless saucepan that you can use to make gravies and soups. A medium-sized pan is great for vegetables and rice and a small pan for heating up milk and boiling eggs. Your saucepans should last you for years. Try to go for nonstick coatings. Start off with a small collection of these four pans and add over time. Stainless steel handles are ideal because they are more durable and you can put them into the oven. Also try to find yourself a large casserole for soups, cooking pasta and making stews.

Frying Pans

A great multipurpose frying pan that can be used for sautéing, stir-fries, pancakes and omelettes is a standard medium size. Opt for a frying pan that has a lid as this will enable you to stop food from bubbling or spitting over your oven top and it speeds up the cooking time too.

Bakeware

You are going to want to be able to make cakes, roast things and bake pies and biscuits. So this means you will need a range of ovenproof tins and trays. You will get an enormous amount of use out of them. Once again, try to go for the best ones you can afford because the thinner, cheaper versions will tend to warp in the heat of the oven. If you can get tins with hardened nonstick surfaces, then these will be invaluable and should last for years. They are also much easier to clean.

Tins and Trays

You will need to buy yourself a large roasting tin. If you can get one with a lid, then all the better. You will be able to use this to cook joints of meat and poultry. You could also use it to bake vegetables and to poach fish. A large baking tray is also essential if you want to make biscuits, cook fish or oven-roast chips or fries. If you are intending to make your own bread, then a large baking tray would do, but you might want to have a loaf tin. Always make sure that your roasting tin in particular is not too wide for your oven. Check, too, that you can move the shelves to accommodate it once it has meat or poultry inside.

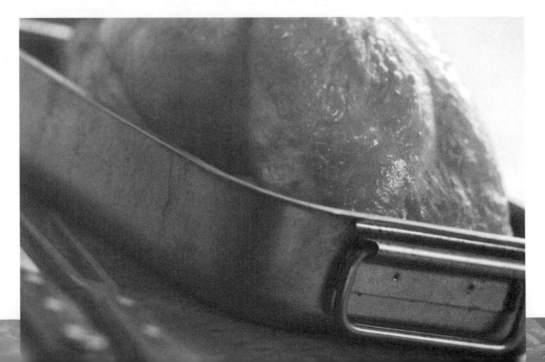

Knives

There is a more bewildering range of knives available on the market compared to almost any other kitchen equipment. You just need to start off with a couple and then gradually increase the collection as you can afford them. With the exception of a good bread knife, you do not need to buy ones with serrated blades. Try to avoid the really cheap knives because they will dull very quickly and they will cause you more work because they are not good enough for the job. Stainless steel, with tough plastic handles, capable of being used and abused and cleaned in a dishwasher are the ideal solution.

Basic Knife Set

To start off your collection of knives, you should certainly consider buying the following items:

- **Cook's knife**: Ideally with a blade around 19 cm/7 in long. A top quality cook's knife might cost you as much as £15/US$20, but it is the most versatile type of knife, enabling quick, fine chopping.

- **Vegetable knife**: Usually with a blade about 10 cm/4 in long.

- **Serrated bread knife**: These make slicing loaves quick and neat.

- **Knife sharpener**: Do not buy a new knife just because your current one has dulled – sharpen it! While a whetstone is the best way to properly sharpen a knife, you could also use a sharpening (or honing) steel, which is less abrasive but will sharpen to a degree and smooth roughness out of the blade.

Measuring Equipment

To get the best from any recipe you will need to be able to measure out the correct quantities of ingredients needed. So you will need measuring scales, jugs, cups and spoons in order to get the best results. It also means that you can use bulk ingredients, rather than buying more expensive packets that have the ingredients ready weighed for convenience.

Scales

Digital scales will give you the most accurate results. Because you might be using recipes from the internet, or a book that has been written in a different country, it would also be handy to have a set of scales that can be switched between metric and imperial. If you can find a set that can also be reset once you have put a bowl or container on them, then this would be ideal and will avoid your having to recalculate each time.

Measuring Jugs

You could weigh liquids and convert them from weight to volume on a set of digital scales. But all you really need is a measuring jug with clearly marked metric and imperial quantities. Try to buy yourself a heavy-duty glass one. These are capable of withstanding very hot liquids and will not discolour. You will also be able to use it in the microwave if you have one. Go for the 2-l/3$\frac{1}{2}$-pt/2-qt version if you are planning to cook in bulk.

Measuring Cups and Spoons

If you live in the US, you will probably measure your ingredients in cups. It is handy to have a full set of measuring cups and millilitre-size mini pans for measuring out those tricky fractions, quarter and half-cup amounts. And everyone should have a set of measuring spoons. You will have noticed that in many of the recipes in this book, there are teaspoon (tsp) or tablespoon (tbsp) measurements. Remember that a 'tablespoon' is bigger than a 'dessert spoon'. Ideally, you will not rely on your table cutlery because these may not be accurate – everyone's teaspoons can differ in size – you can buy a plastic, double-ended measuring spoon, which will be far more accurate.

Utensils

There is a good variety of different kitchen utensils on offer. The truth is, you only need a few of them. If you have invested in nonstick pans, make sure that you buy cooking utensils that are made from heat-resistant but non-metallic materials so that they will not scratch the nonstick surfaces, ruining your pans for ever.

Wooden Spoons and Spatulas

Really, you need a minimum of two wooden spoons. You need to keep these clean, and as soon as they become discoloured or are cracked replace them. So it does not pay to buy expensive ones. A flexible, plastic spatula is great for scraping the sides of pans and mixing bowls. A stepped spatula can help you move foods between dishes and is great for flipping omelettes.

Ladles, Balloon Whisks and Potato Mashers

You will need a ladle to serve soups and stews. You only really need one ladle, so go for a medium-sized one. Balloon whisks are used for whisking up cream and eggs and are also essential for creating smooth sauces. Another useful item is a potato masher, which can be used to mash any sort of vegetable or fruit. Try to find one that has a rounded, plastic end, as this will protect your pans.

Kitchen Scissors and Tongs

You need a pair of robust, sharp and fairly large kitchen scissors. You will need them for a variety of jobs, from trimming meat and fish to snipping herbs, and to cut greaseproof paper to fit into your pans or your preserving jars. Try to find a pair where the handles separate to make cleaning far easier. Tongs are also useful for turning foods over in a pan or roasting tin and for transferring food from the tin or pan on to the plate.

Can Opener, Vegetable Peeler and Grater

You do not need a wall-mounted, electric can opener, or anything particularly fancy. Just find one that feels comfortable in your hand and has a good grip. It also needs to have a nice smooth turning mechanism. The best type of vegetable peeler to use is a y-shaped peeler. This will allow you to peel your vegetables very quickly, taking off a very thin layer and giving you an even look. For grating, try to find the four-sided kind, as these are really versatile. You will be able to grate from coarse to extremely fine, so they are ideal for grating lemon rind, chocolate, cheese and nutmeg.

Colander, Sieve and Mixing Bowls

A colander is used for washing vegetables and salad and for draining cooked vegetables, rice and pasta. To wash, simply place the produce into the colander and run them under a cold tap. To sift lumps out of flour or cocoa or to wash fine-grained foods, try to find a fine mesh sieve. You can also use it for sauces and soups to get that smooth finish. Mixing bowls are great to prepare, mix and store food. Go for ones that can be used either in the microwave or in the oven and that you can stack inside one another so that they take up less storage space. If you can find ones with lids, even better.

Chopping Boards

Although wooden chopping/cutting boards are very popular and have their advantages (see page 94), white polyethylene boards are very lightweight and perfectly hygienic as long as you clean them well. Try to buy two and go for different colours. Use one for raw meat and fish and the other for your vegetables, fruit and salads. This will cut down on bacterial cross-contamination hazards. If you really want to, buy a red one for meat, blue for fish and green for vegetables.

Electrical Equipment

You can cope in the kitchen without a single electrical gadget. However, there are some kitchen appliances that are not only very useful, but will also take a lot of the time and effort out of routine and repetitive kitchen tasks. Like many electrical products, it does not often pay in the long run to buy the cheapest you can find. It may not last very long, it is usually underpowered and it is often incredibly difficult to get repaired or to find spare parts. Watch out for them in the sales and then decide to invest.

Kettle

One of the biggest problems with kettles is that we tend to overfill them. Buy one that shows you how much water is inside, so you only ever boil what you need. It is also worth buying a cordless kettle. This makes life far easier and allows you to move the kettle to where you are working if you need freshly boiled water for your food. Rapid-boil kettles can boil two cups of water in less than 60 seconds, but this is not really essential. Although it depends on taste, stainless steel kettles are often easier to maintain and keep clean. You will get a limescale build-up, so make sure that the water filter near the spout is regularly cleaned and use neat white vinegar, which you boil in the kettle, to de-scale it.

Microwave

For many households, microwaves revolutionized cooking. The first one was built in the US in 1947 and was massive. It cost US$5,000. Microwaves are certainly useful, although it has to be said they are not essential – despite the fact that many people would say they could not manage without one! Not only can they be used for cooking and steaming, but also for defrosting. They are great for reheating a second meal if you have cooked in bulk. They are also money-saving because of the reduction in cooking time and thus the amount of energy used.

Hand Blender

These are often known as stick blenders. Some come with whisk attachments and others have extra attachments that can rule out having to buy an electric whisk or a chopper. The cheap ones have less power and tend to wear out quite quickly. Hand blenders are great for:

- soups, smoothies and milkshakes
- whisking egg whites and cream
- preparing baby foods or purees
- fine chopping

Slow Cooker

Although these are not essential, they are brilliant labour-saving devices and allow you to make pot roasts, stews and other dishes. If you are a working couple, you can prepare your one-pot dish and then leave the slow cooker to do its work while you head off for yours. They come in a variety of sizes, from a capacity of 500 ml/18 fl oz/2 cups to 7 l/12 pt/7 qt. Slow cookers can have a number of temperature settings, from high to 'keep warm'. They are safe to leave unattended all day or right through the night.

Equipment You Could Do Without

We have already seen that you do not actually need to buy any electrical equipment at all. But if you are intending to spend any time in the kitchen and save money by preparing your own meals, then you might want to consider gradually investing in a range of electrical, labour-saving devices. Do not be seduced into believing that you really need them, however. Mainly they are time-savers and do not necessarily improve the quality of what you are producing.

Juicer

Juicers are far more compact and elegant-looking than the enormous devices that were incredibly difficult to clean out when they first arrived on the market. Basically, a juicer squeezes all of the fluids out of fruit or vegetables. Admittedly, this is difficult to do by hand; imagine how long it would take to squeeze the juice out of a carrot. Soft fruits, however, can easily be turned into juice without a juicer; all you need is a hand juicer or a masher and a bowl.

Smoothie Maker

A smoothie maker is just like a juicer, except it finely chops and shreds the fruit and vegetables. Again, this can be difficult if not impossible to do by hand. However, smoothies are usually premium priced products in the store, so if you are addicted to them, then a smoothie maker might make it on to your essential electrical equipment list. Bear in mind, though, the time involved and the cost of the fresh fruit in the first place.

Coffee Maker

Espresso makers, filter-coffee makers, cappuccino makers, latte makers and coffee percolators can produce that perfect cup of coffee and that unbeatable aroma. But they do have their disadvantages. They are expensive and they are time consuming, not just to use but also to keep clean. If you do not drink the filter coffee fresh, it tastes badly stewed. Go for a traditional coffee percolator or a cafetière if you like ground coffee.

Bread Maker

There must be tens or hundreds of thousands of unused bread makers around the world. You simply follow the recipe in the guidebook, dropping in the dry and wet ingredients and press a button and, hey presto, in two hours or so, you have got a fresh steaming loaf of bread. The bread maker mixes, proves, rises and bakes your loaf. However, it also takes out a lot of the pleasure of making your own bread and, with the amount of energy it has used, you probably could have bought a loaf.

Food Processor

Food processors seem to be able to do everything except eat the food for you. They can chop, juice, slice, dice, shred, blend and mix. But so can you! Some people like the even consistency that food processors produce. But there is nothing quite like the more rough and ready rustic look that you can produce on your own chopping board. What is more, food processors can be incredibly expensive and hard to come to grips with and they take up an enormous amount of valuable cupboard or shelf space.

Toaster and Sandwich Toaster

What is wrong with the grill/broiler in your oven? Toasters – despite seeming an essential item to many of us – often give you uneven colouration on the bread. And sandwich toasters produce super-heated cheese and burning tomato. Using the grill will allow you to make perfectly good toasted sandwiches, open or closed. Just make sure you lay a sheet of kitchen foil under the grill tray and this will help reflect heat back to speed up cooking and keep your grill tray free of burnt-on cheese.

Dishwasher

OK, so it is a chore, having to hand wash all the plates, pots and pans, kitchen utensils and cutlery after your meal. But you do not need a dishwasher. It might be nice to have one, but you do not need it. Of course you can use lower-temperature settings, but the problem is that the dishwasher will not cut through the grease and clean properly. Dishwashers use a lot of water, plenty of detergent and energy and you need to keep it clean and have special plumbing fitted for the waste water, not to mention the cost of the salt and the rinse aid needed (or the equally pricey 3-in-1 tablets).

Where to Buy Kitchen Equipment

At any given time, eBay alone has tens of thousands of cooking items on offer. But you can find decent cooking equipment in a wide variety of stores and markets. Often, they are on offer in your regular grocery store or in department stores. Great places to look for your basic equipment are the discount stores, which often have end-of-line ranges. Some of the larger chain stores have their own cook shops and will sometimes have special promotions.

Pots, Pans and Bakeware

If your budget is limited, then go for the minimum number of pots, pans and bakeware that were outlined earlier. It is better to spend more on a few than it is to spread your money by buying a large set of cheap items. They will not last and they are a false economy. Look for special offers in chain stores or complete boxed sets in your grocery store. Often, the sets are discounted and have all the basic items that you will need. Make sure you have a look at them, feel their weight and quality before you buy.

Utensils

For your utensils, the cheapest are the bamboo or wooden varieties, closely followed by nylon and then the more expensive stainless steel and metal varieties. As these items are relatively cheap, you can economize by buying the cheaper varieties and replacing them from time to time as they wear out. You will also quickly discover which ones you use the most. The utensil sets tend to have all the major items, but some of them you will rarely use, like apple corers. Buy yourself a nice, decorative pot to put all your utensils in and then shop around for bargains. Try chain stores, discount stores and market stalls.

Electrical Goods

Trendy new kitchen gadgets, with the latest designs, can be ridiculously expensive and they can go out of fashion very quickly. You do not need to buy branded electrical goods. The only advantage is that they often have good after-sales service and you can buy spare parts. The price of basic electrical items has tumbled. You do not need to pay that much for a microwave or a blender. So shop around. Department stores and electrical specialist stores often have special offers and you can get great bargains in discount stores. Do not be tempted to buy second hand: you do not know what kind of treatment it has had in the past.

Storage

Storing food and keeping it edible is an age-old concern for humans. Periods of plenty and scarcity go with the seasons and humans have searched for centuries for ways to safely store their food and keep it safe until they need it. We all know just how much food goes to waste, these days – upwards of thirty per cent of everything we buy ends up thrown away or on the compost heap. Just think – how much are you wasting each year? Storage means organization, rotation and inventory keeping and not to mention a little effort – but it is worth it.

Ways to Prolong the Life of Food

Being able to stock up on food when it is cheap is great, but the problem is, do you really want to be eating beetroot with every meal for the next month? Well, of course, it does not have to be like that as there are various ways of prolonging the shelf life of food: you can freeze, dry, 'can', preserve or vacuum-seal vegetables, meats, herbs and grains. Preserving can be complicated and you need special equipment, but it might be worth your while in the long run as we will see – for centuries, humans have been drying their food to preserve it. You can dehydrate, smoke, sun-dry, air-dry or bake and get the same effect.

The Ancient Art of Freezing

The freezing process stops the chemical and biological processes that slowly break down food. These days, most of us have a freezer, so freezing has got to be one of the easiest ways of preserving the freshness of food. Nearly every type of food is capable of being frozen, but some work better than others. Get it right and sweetcorn or peas can taste as good as the day they were picked. Do not try it with lettuce or raw potatoes, there is just too much water in them. Some foods are preserved better by freezing if you blanch or even cook them first. At the very least, you should always clean fruit and vegetables before freezing.

Freezing Vegetables

Some vegetables will need a certain amount of preparation before freezing. Blanching consists of immersing the vegetables in boiling water for a short period of time. You can use plastic boxes instead of freezer bags, but always allow space in the box because the vegetables will expand when they are frozen. Never forget to label and date your frozen packages, making sure that you use a waterproof pen. Here are some tips on how to prepare certain vegetables before freezing them:

- **Green beans**: Cut off the ends and cut the beans in half, then blanch for 3 minutes.

- **Beetroot**: Fully cook it (for 30–45 minutes).

- **Broccoli**: Trim and rinse, cut small and blanch for 3 minutes.

- **Carrots**: Peel and cut, then blanch for 2–5 minutes.

- **Corn on the cob**: Cook for 7–11 minutes.

- **Mushrooms**: Trim, slice and sauté. Let them cool before freezing.

- **Onions**: Peel and chop, then freeze.

- **Peas**: Shell and freeze on a tray, then put into bags.

- **Tomatoes**: Scald in water, peel off skins, then heat through and freeze once cool.

Drying

Drying has got to be one of the oldest ways of preserving food. Simply, it means taking out the moisture from the food. This is the important part as it means starving the micro-organisms in the food of the moisture they need to thrive. When they are dried out, the fruits and vegetables will only have around 10 per cent of their moisture left in them. The great thing about drying is that it does not destroy the nutrients in the food like heating does. To eat the food, all that is necessary is to add water again. We routinely eat dried produce such as raisins (dried grapes), prunes (dried plums), coffee and most of the spices we use.

Simple Dehydration

Dehydrators have tumbled in price. Check out the internet or department stores. Not all of the dehydrators will dry out at the same speed, always check the manual. Also, make sure that the food is properly spaced. Leave a space between each item because stacking can mean that the drying process takes longer. Make sure you get a dehydrator with:

- a reasonable price
- enough capacity
- light and sturdy trays
- simple controls

Sun-drying

Ideally, choose a hot and still day when there is little or no moisture in the air. A screen can be made up from an old window frame or picture frame. Stretch some cotton sheeting over the frame (cheesecloth will also do). Secure with tacks. Place the fruit or vegetables on a rack under the screen; make sure there is room for the air to circulate. It will take around 4 days for them to be thoroughly dried out. Make sure you take them in at night as there will be more moisture in the air. To make sure that the produce is thoroughly dry and bug-free, heat it up for 10 to 15 minutes in a hot oven and then pack into an airtight container.

Smoking

Many people make their own smokers, but commercial ones are not that expensive. They comprise a metal unit within which you can put hickory, charcoal or wood chips that are slowly burned to produce smoke. The smoke heats up and infuses the meat with a smoky flavour. You will need two thermometers – one for the food and one for the heater. The temperature in the heater needs to be between 107°C/225°F and 150°C/300°F. Make sure that both of the thermometers are ovenproof. Once the meat is cooled down, freeze it. Otherwise, make sure you use it within four days.

Safe Smoking

It is not easy to be precise about the temperature that the meat needs to reach because it depends on its size and shape and how far away it is from the source of the heat. It could take up to eight hours to smoke meat; the following list gives you some guide to temperatures.

- poultry (breast) – 80°C/170°F
- poultry (whole) – 85°C/180°F
- beef, lamb or veal joint – 65–80°C/145–175°F
- pork joint – 70°C–80°C/160–170°F

Smoking Fish

Preserving fish by smoking has been practised for many centuries. Cold smoking needs temperatures of around 27°C/80°F and hot smoking needs 94°C/200°F. You will first need to make some brine as the fish needs to soak in the brine for 15 minutes for every 1.3 cm/½ in to cure it. Use 2½ tablespoons plain salt per 250 ml/8 fl oz/1 cup water. Then, it can actually take several days for the cold smoking of fish, but hot smoking need only take a few hours. The longer the fish is smoked, the more it will absorb the smoke flavour.

Smoked Trout

This is straightforward, with a preparation time of 10 minutes and a smoking time of 3 hours:

- prepare your trout by gutting them
- stuff the trout with sliced lemon and a clove of garlic
- grind some black pepper over the trout
- place in the smoker for 3 hours
- when finished, remove the stuffing and serve, or freeze for later use

Vacuum Sealing

In vacuum sealing, the food is put into a heavy plastic wrapping and the air is literally sucked out and the food sealed in, which extends the shelf life of food. This offers enormous potential savings. To do it, you need a small machine, but they need not cost more than around £40/US$55 and the bags are available in a variety of different sizes. They extract the moisture and air, so that the food can be kept in the bags for a considerable period of time. You can even use them to make your own boil-in-the-bag meals and keep them in the freezer until you want to use them.

Preserving

Preserving in glass jars (also known as 'canning') is a great way of prolonging the life of food. Heat needs to be used in the process to kill off harmful micro-organisms, so it is important to get things right. Ideally, produce needs to be eaten within a year. This means that you can enjoy summer fruits all through the winter, then stock up again the next year when the prices tumble again. It is a relatively simple process, but you will need some fairly inexpensive equipment. Most importantly, to make it worthwhile, you will need to have plenty of produce ready to can and a few hours set aside to get the job done.

Preserving - What You'll Need

All you really need is to start collecting empty jars. Clean them and collect them as you use them; screw-top jars are the best, particularly those with plastic on the inside of the jar lid. You can buy empty jam jars or special preserving jars, but these are not really necessary. You will also need some greaseproof paper, cutting out circles to fit the jars as you will be dropping these into the jars on top of the produce. These inhibit the growth of mould and stop a thick film forming at the top of the jar.

Preserving - Getting Started

Now that you have a good collection of jars and matching lids, put the jars into a hot oven to sterilize them. Ideally, when you start putting the produce into the jars; the glass should be very hot in order to dissuade bacteria. Be careful with the lids too; do not try to sterilize plastic lids in the oven (or metal ones with plastic inserts!). Lay out everything you will be using and give yourself plenty of space. Firstly, wash the fruit or vegetables. Now you are ready to start putting the food into the jars.

Preserving - Next Step

Fill the jars with the fruit or vegetables, but not to the very top – make sure that the food is not going to be touching the lid of the jar. You can either pack in the fruit or vegetables raw or you can put them in ready cooked. Once the jars are full, for fruit, fill the jar with either syrup or fruit juice, and for vegetables, boiling water or salted water. Allow for expansion, so leave some space in the neck of the jar. Now put the lids on and label the jars once they have cooled down. Make sure you tighten them up once more before storing.

Making Your Own Jam

To take advantage of seasonal gluts in fruit, it is a great idea to make your own jam. You will need:

 a preserving pan or a large stainless-steel pan

 clean jars with lids

ready-cut greaseproof paper circles the size of the jar

labels

What Will Set and What Will Not?

One of the problems is making sure that your jam will set. Sometimes you will need a little pectin, but you can easily add a little fruit juice or lemon juice to get this. You can break fruits down into three different categories, by their willingness to set:

 Fruit that will easily set: Apples, blackcurrants, gooseberries, plums, damsons and redcurrants

Fruit that may need a little pectin: Apricots, raspberries, blackberries and loganberries

 Fruit that will definitely need pectin: Cherries and strawberries

Quantities

Generally, it is reckoned that you will get 2.25 kg/5 lb of jam for every 1.36 kg/3 lb of sugar you use. Fill your jam jars with water and then pour the water into your pan. You can now see how much volume is going to be needed to fill those jars. This is a useful precaution to make sure that you do not make too much or too little jam to fill your jars.

Making Strawberry Jam

You will need:

 1.6 kg/3½ lb/11⅓ cups hulled strawberries
juice of 1 lemon
1.36 kg/3 lb/7 cups white sugar

Heat up the strawberries and lemon juice in the pan. Then add the sugar, stirring until it is dissolved. Boil until the setting point is reached. Remove any scum, then leave it to cool until a skin forms. Stir, then place in the jars. To test whether setting point has been reached, when your jam has ceased frothing and it is less noisy when it is boiling, remove the pan from the heat, put a little of the jam on to a cold plate or saucer and let it cool. If the setting point has been reached, the surface of the jam will set and it will wrinkle when you push it with your finger. If it does not wrinkle, return the pan to the heat and continue to boil. Test again in 5 minutes.

Making Your Own Chutney

Chutney can be a delicious accompaniment to hot or cold meats and is also good in sandwiches. It also gives you the chance to use a mixture of fruit and vegetables in the same recipe when they are plentiful. What is more, you can enjoy the chutney for months to come. Some chutneys can be complicated to make and it is even possible to make your own tomato ketchup, which is a form of chutney.

Apple Chutney

This recipe for apple chutney allows you to take advantage of a seasonal glut in apples and onions. You will need the same items (pan, jars, paper, labels) as listed above for making jam. Ideally, use cooking apples and white onions, rather than eating apples or red onions. You will need:

- 1.36 kg/3 lb/6 cups cooking apples, peeled, cored and chopped
- 450 g/1 lb/4 cups white onions, peeled and finely sliced
- 680 g/1¹/₂ lb/3¹/₂ cups white sugar
- 220 g/¹/₂ lb/1 cup sultanas
- 125 g/4 oz preserved ginger
- 300 ml/¹/₂ pint/1¹/₄ cups white vinegar
- 1 tbsp salt
- ¹/₂ tsp ground black pepper

Put the apples and onions together with the vinegar and all the ingredients except the sugar into your large pan. Stir well over a medium heat until the apples begin to break down. Now add the sugar and stir in until it has dissolved. Boil steadily until the chutney has the consistency of thick jam. Use the plate test if you are unsure if the chutney is ready. Pour the chutney into hot jars and seal them immediately. Label when cool.

Storing Food

Although it can be a great deal of fun filling up a shopping trolley, you are often faced with the difficulty of finding room for its contents and putting it in the right place when you get back home. Hopefully, you have not come back from your grocery shop with anything you did not intend to buy. Your sorting out and storage, however, should begin at the checkout. Sort out your dry goods, cans, vegetables and other items and put them into different bags. Also, make sure that you do not put fragile foods at the bottom of the bag where they could get squashed.

Once You Get Home

Obviously, you need to put the frozen food and fresh produce away in the freezer or the fridge as soon as you can. Apples, bananas and citrus fruits, you can easily store in a fruit bowl, but not near the oven or exposed to direct sunlight. If you have bought bananas, keep them away from the other fruit because they will encourage the other fruit to ripen very quickly.

Vegetables

If you are not storing your vegetables in the fridge, then they should be kept in a cool, dark place. Vegetables begin losing their vitamin content straight after they have been harvested and the longer you keep them, the fewer nutrients they will have. Vegetables are best bought on a regular basis, in small amounts. Frozen vegetables do keep their vitamins, so frozen veg is often a good idea.

Meat, Poultry and Fish

These items definitely need to go straight into the fridge or the freezer. You should really try to keep separate shelves for these at the bottom of your fridge. Make sure you rotate so that the older items are at the front and you use them first. If you have bought a value pack of chicken breasts, for example, and only want to use two of them, it is much easier to separate them before you freeze them. Take them out and wrap them separately in clingfilm before freezing them.

Fridge Organization

Does your ice taste of garlic and have you always got limp lettuce? If so, then you really need to reorganize your fridge. Fridges do not make food cold; they remove the heat and moisture, just like an air conditioner. That is a good reason for not leaving food or drinks uncovered. Here are some other pointers:

 Fresh eggs: Eggs are best kept in their cartons because they lose moisture through their shells.

 Crisp lettuce: Watery foods like lettuce stay crisper if they are wrapped in a plastic bag, trapping the moisture.

Peak Efficiency

Your fridge should be set at around 3°C/37°F. You can always buy a fridge thermometer to keep a check on this, but do not over freeze your fridge. It will not only cost you more in energy, but will damage your food. Always try to keep your fridge at least three quarters full rather than almost empty. This is because, when you open the door, warm air will rush in and, if there are plenty of cold things in the fridge, the temperature will remain more stable. But do not pack things in too tightly because the air will not be able to circulate.

Fridge Contents Management

You should, of course, clean your fridge regularly. Make a habit of throwing out old food at least once a week. Get rid of old ice, as it will have picked up odours. If you are going to give your fridge a thorough clean, then make sure you unplug it first. A few times a year, you should also pull your fridge out and vacuum the dust and hair off the condenser at the back. This will stop it from overheating.

Allocating Shelf Space

Divide your space up on the shelves of your fridge. Group similar items, such as beverages and dairy products, together. Make sure you rotate perishable foods, check your dates and dispose of anything that you are unsure about. You should keep meat, poultry and fish towards the bottom of your fridge. Put the items that you use most frequently at the front of the shelves. Cover everything because foods left uncovered can take on the flavour of odours in the fridge.

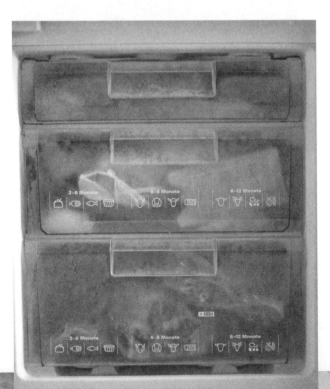

Freezer

We have seen how important it is to put frozen food straight into your freezer as soon as you arrive home, but this often means just throwing them in and burying items for ever. You might need to use a fast-freeze button if you are putting in joints of meat or whole poultry. Luckily, many of the more modern freezers automatically turn off the fast-freeze after a few hours, but check. Ideally, your freezer should be set at -23°C/-10°F.

Organizing Your Chest Freezer

These types of freezer are notoriously difficult to organize and they can either be too crowded, which will affect the air circulation, or too empty, which means they are not energy efficient. If you have a large chest freezer, consider buying some cheap plastic boxes, or even using cardboard boxes, to organize and stack your food. You should run a 'first in, first out' policy for all of your frozen items. It is so easy to lose track of what you have got and how long it has been there. A great solution is to fix a small notebook to a magnet and place it on your freezer. You can record when you froze items and when they should be consumed.

Upright Freezers

Upright freezers have their advantages and disadvantages. They have baskets, wire racks and shelves, so you can keep your meat, poultry, vegetables and desserts all separate. This should make them far easier to find. The problem is, of course, that things could get shoved to the back of the baskets or shelves and forgotten. It is a good idea to sort out your freezer at least every six months. Check everything and, if you have labelled it, you will know just how long it has been in there and whether or not it is still edible.

Cupboards

Try to keep cupboards or areas in cupboards set aside for particular things. By doing this, you can easily see what you have got left in stock and be able to go straight to it when you need it for cooking. Ideally, group items as follows:

- **cereals**
- **cans**
- **oils**
- **condiments and sauces**
- **rice and pasta**

Tea, Coffee and Sugar/Sweeteners

If you have got a cupboard over or near the kettle, store these with your mugs and cups. This should make them all far more accessible because these are items that you will use most often in the kitchen. You can always have additional stores of these items in your lower cupboards, but remember to check before you restock at the grocery store. You could keep a pot of teaspoons beside the kettle to speed things up when you are making a hot drink.

Eye Level

If it is possible, you should try to put your cans and dried goods in a cupboard that is at eye level, so it is easier to find what you are looking for. You can always have your main stock of these items elsewhere and then top up the eye-level storage as and when you need to. Rice and pasta is best kept in large storage jars because it is easy to see how much you have left. Keep your bread in a bread bin because it prevents crumbs from getting all over the worktops and your bread will stay fresher for longer.

Plastic Boxes

A set of plastic boxes with lids is a great and cheap investment, as long as they are airtight. You can store cereals, grains and pulses, nuts, flour and pasta in these. Buy stackable ones and, even better, buy those with write-on, wipe off labels.

Other containers

Seasonal gifts like boxes of biscuits, confectionery and cakes can provide you with a ready and free selection of tins and other containers. Use them for your own home-made biscuits and cakes. Once again, these containers need to be airtight to do their job right. You can improve the sealing quality by stretching clingfilm over the open tin before replacing the lid.

Cooking for Beginners

PACKED WITH MONEY SAVING IDEAS & TIPS

Basic Techniques

The challenges of cooking on a daily basis and making sure we eat well can seem daunting. If you are new to cooking, then you may not be familiar with the basic techniques, so learning them is a great alternative to expensive and tiny ready meals, dodgy takeaways and fatty and sugar-high snack foods. You do not have to be a trained chef to cook a good, nourishing meal, any more than you have to be well-off to eat. You can easily prepare good food by following just a few of the basic techniques.

Fish

Fish is rich in protein. Oily fish, such as salmon, herring and mackerel, is rich in vitamins A and D. White fish has very little fat. Canned fish is often packed in oil, which adds fat. The tiny bones are actually soft enough to be eaten and they contain calcium and phosphorous. Many of the basic techniques we will talk about relate to fresh sea and freshwater fish, as these are often as cheap, if not cheaper, than frozen varieties.

Spotting a Good Fish

These are points to look out for when buying fresh fish:

- **Texture**: The flesh should be firm and not flabby.

- **Odour**: No stale or unpleasant odour should be present.

- **Gills**: These should be bright red in most varieties.

- **Eyes**: The fish's eyes should be bright and not sunken-in and dull.

- **Skin**: The skin should be slimy, but not have a yellowish slime, as this shows the fish has begun to rot.

Buying Your Fish

Do not go out intending to buy a certain kind of fish. Buy what is in season and is plentiful and cheap. The price of fish varies even greater than most other types of food. Because it is so perishable, sometimes particular fish are very scarce and at other times there is far more available than can be sold. Go for smaller, younger fish. A flatfish, for example, should be thick in proportion to its size. Always choose a thick slice from a small fish rather than a thin slice from a larger one. This will mean that more of what you buy will be edible and not bone or waste.

Fresh Fish

Ideally, you should cook your fresh fish on the same day as you buy it. It quickly loses its freshness and flavour. If you are going to put it in your fridge, then make sure you cover it, otherwise it will taint the other food. If frozen fish has thawed out, never refreeze it, so check whether the 'fresh fish' from the fishmonger, fish stall or grocery store is fresh or whether it has previously been frozen.

Preparing a Whole Fish

The first thing you will have to do is scrape off the scales with the back of a knife: scrape from the tail towards the head whilst holding the fish's tail, and rinse the fish whilst you work as this will remove the loose scales. When cutting, use a pair of kitchen scissors or a sharp knife. To deal with mackerel, trout, salmon and other round fish like cod, slit the belly from just below the head to halfway to the tail and remove the entrails. Then wash the fish inside and out and rub in some salt to remove any black tissue. If you want to take the head off, cut across the fish just behind the gills.

To deal with flatfish, you need to cut off the fins, remove the gills, open up the belly (just under the head), remove and discard the entrails and wash the fish out under cold water. To remove the head, make a semicircular cut below the head.

Skinning Fish

Both flat and round fish need to be wet before you skin them. For round fish:

- cut a strip of skin along the backbone, near the tail
- make a second cut just below the head
- loosen this skin with a sharp knife
- dip your fingers into salt for a better grip
- gently pull the skin, working towards the tail
- keep your thumb pressed over the backbone to prevent the flesh from coming away

For a flatfish:

- begin at the tail
- cut the skin across but do not cut into the flesh
- loosen the skin around the fins with your fingers
- tear off the skin, keeping your thumb pressed against the backbone

Filleting Fish

A fillet is just a whole piece of the fish, from the shoulder to the tail. You can get four fillets from a flatfish and two from a round fish. For a round fish:

 slit the fish down the centre to the bone

working from the head to the tail, cut along the belly

cut the flesh away from the bones, keeping the knife pressed against the bone

For a flatfish:

 cut the flesh from head to tail along the backbone using a sharp, flexible knife

 push your knife into the slit and separate the flesh from the bone

remove the fillet, turn the fish around and take the second fillet out

repeat for the other side of the fish

Cooking Fish

It is very easy to over- or undercook fish. You need to check the thickest part of your fish and see whether the flesh will easily come away from the bones after cooking. If you are cooking fillets, a white curd will be visible between the flakes, showing you that it is cooked. There are plenty of different ways to cook fish, including boiling and poaching, steaming, grilling/broiling and frying, but you can also stew or bake.

Frying Fish

Before you fry fish, make sure it is dry. Ideally, coat the fish to stop fat from being absorbed into it. You can simply do this by rolling the fish in a little flour. To fry, there needs to be enough oil to come halfway up the fish. Heat up the oil and then carefully place the fish into the pan. Fry until it is golden brown on one side and then turn the fish. You will need 6–8 minutes for fillets and 8–12 minutes for whole fish.

Poaching Fish

You should never boil a fish: you simmer a fish. You can use a deep frying pan or a wide saucepan and cook the fish in just enough water to cover it. You can add vinegar, salt or lemon juice to the water. Lemon juice in particular will make sure that white fish retains its colour. When boiling point is reached, reduce the heat and, although cooking time depends on the thickness of the fish, you should allow 10–15 minutes per 450 g/1 lb of fish. Fish can also be poached in milk, wine or cider, or a combination of those with water.

Grilling/Broiling Fish

This is a much healthier alternative to frying, but, if it is not an oily fish, it is a good idea to brush a little olive oil over the fish's flesh and season with salt and pepper. If you score the fish with a sharp knife before cooking, then this will prevent it from burning on the outside and being uncooked on the inside. Heat the grill and rub a little oil on the rack to stop the fish from sticking. Grill on a low heat, turning the fish occasionally. It will take 7–8 minutes for a fillet and 10–15 minutes for thicker steaks.

Steaming Fish

This is a slower process than poaching but it keeps more of the fish's natural flavour. Wrap your whole fish, after seasoning it, in greaseproof paper. Place the wrapped fish in your steamer, above a pan of boiling water. Put the lid on top of the steamer and steam for between 10–25 minutes, depending on how thick your fish is. The greaseproof paper will protect your fish and it will mean that the skin is stuck to the paper and not to the steamer.

Stewing and Baking Fish

Stewing cooks the fish by gently simmering in the stew liquid. It is ideal for large chunks of fish. You can stew in either milk or water, which has been seasoned, and you can add a variety of vegetables of your choice. Cook it rather like a casserole: in a dish in the oven. The other oven option is to bake the fish. Prepare your fish and put it into a well-greased baking tin or dish. Cover your fish in greased baking parchment. You will need to use a fairly hot oven, but it will only take around 20 minutes to cook.

Meat and Poultry

Meat and poultry are incredibly versatile foods. They come in a bewildering range of different cuts. You can boil, roast, fry, barbecue, smoke or pickle. You can stew, dry or even make hamburgers, meatballs, sausages and pies with meat and poultry. Meat is high in protein and provides many of the essential amino acids we need. It is low in carbohydrate and can be high in fat, depending on the meat and the cut. Meat is probably the most expensive food item, but bargains can be had and wholesome meals can be made that can be stretched quite easily.

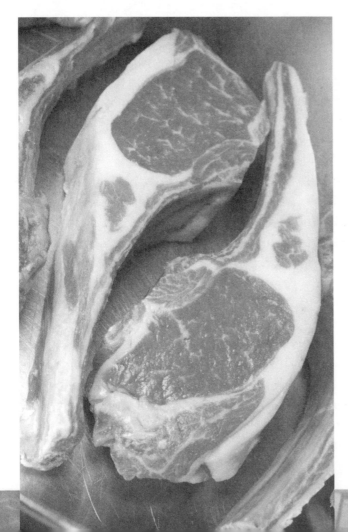

Pork

Originally, pork was cured to preserve it and so bacon, ham and gammon, sausages and salami were all created. Most of these types of pork are cured in some way, perhaps by smoking or drying. But there is as wide a variety of different cuts of pork as there are beef and lamb. Pork can be roasted, grilled/broiled, fried, braised, stewed and casseroled or pot-roasted. Pork has a mild flavour and it is great with fruits and vegetables, particularly apples and red cabbage. Herbs that work well with pork include sage, rosemary and thyme. But also try ginger, allspice or nutmeg. Either rub it in dry or make yourself a simple marinade.

Choosing Pork

Most pigs are brought to market at around six months old, so the cuts should be moist and pink and not red or grey. Find cuts that have a fine-grain texture. There may be some marbling. If you spot free range, organic or rare-breed pork on special offer, it is really worth trying it. The pigs are reared in much more natural conditions and, as a result, the meat is far more tasty.

Roasting Pork

Pork joints are best cooked with the distinctive crackling, or layer of fat, wrapped around them. You should score and salt this fat before transferring the joint into a roasting tin. Pork will need around 25 minutes for every 450 g/1 lb. To get the best crackling, put the pork in the oven at the highest temperature you have for the first 20 minutes, then turn your oven down to 180°C/350°F/Gas Mark 4 for the remainder of the required cooking time. Let the pork rest for around 15 minutes before you carve it. You can roast rib, belly or shoulder joints for roast pork dinners.

Cheapest Cuts of Pork

Amongst the cheapest cuts of pork are:

 Belly: Great for casseroles, barbecuing, braising and slow roasting.

Hock: Ideal for soups, stews, casseroles and braised dishes. Although good for flavour, it is not very meaty.

 Shoulder: Great for roasting or can be cut into cubes for casseroles and kebabs.

Minced/ground pork: Usually made from pork shoulder, mince can be used to make meatballs but is also good stir-fried, or even used in any recipe where you would normally use beef mince.

Caribbean Pork

This simple recipe gives you a chance to get some of your herbs out of the store cupboard.
You will need:

- 1.3 kg/3 lb belly joint
- 1 tbsp each ground cumin, chilli powder, ground coriander
- 1 tsp each ground red chilli, ground black pepper, ground cinnamon, brown sugar
- $\frac{1}{2}$ tsp salt

Heat the oven to 180°C/350°F/Gas Mark 4. Mix all of the dry ingredients together and then rub the mixture over the skin of the joint. Put the joint into your roasting tin and roast for $1\frac{1}{2}$ to 2 hours. Remove from the oven, cover with kitchen foil and allow to rest for 10 minutes before cutting and serving. To make use of the oven, you could serve this with roasted vegetables. Slice up whatever you have into similar sized chunks. Drizzle over some olive oil, rosemary and salt. Cover with kitchen foil and cook until golden.

Lamb

Lamb can be extremely expensive. Technically, 'lamb' is no more than 1 year old; after that, a lamb is called a 'hogget', which is defined by having no more than two permanent incisors in wear. After that point, it must be sold as mutton, which is considerably cheaper as it is less popular. Most of the mutton comes from breeding animals that are no longer productive in flock. Early lamb may be tender, but as the animal gets older, the meat develops more flavour.

Choosing Lamb

The highest quality lamb has creamy white fat. If it looks crumbly, brittle or yellow, this is from an older animal. The colour of the flesh will depend on where the sheep was raised. Pale pink flesh indicates a young lamb and older animals are darker red. If you are buying a larger cut and it is covered with a white membrane, you should remove this before cooking. Mutton is rich brown in colour; avoid yellow fat and grey meat.

Cooking Lamb

Because lamb is so tender, nearly all the different cooking methods can be used. Marinating lamb is particularly effective. Lamb is used in many different cuisines to create rich, spicy stews, rice dishes and kebabs. Many Indian recipes use mutton. Lamb is also great for a combination of cooking methods. In Greece, it is used in moussaka, in Turkey for koftas. Minced lamb also makes wonderfully juicy burgers, not to mention the classic Shepherd's Pie (*see* page 216).

Cheapest Cuts of Lamb

Breast is one of the cheapest cuts. It is versatile, you can roast it, stuff it, mince it, make kebabs from it and it is ideal for barbecues. The neck is ideal for stewing. The scrag end, or neck, is a tough cut and cheap. Chop it or dice it and use it in stews and casseroles. The shoulder is good for slow roasting and very economical. Get the butcher to leave the blade bone in. If you roast it really slowly at 180°C/350°F/Gas Mark 4 for about 3–4 hours, the meat will fall off the bone. Use strong herbs like rosemary and thyme, olive oil and garlic to flavour the lamb. Put some onion and water into your pot and keep it covered with kitchen foil throughout the cooking time. Also, do not forget that lamb mince will be one of the cheapest 'cuts' available to buy too.

Lamb Shashlik

Here is a great lamb kebab recipe for you to try out. You will need:

- **700 g/1½ lb lamb, from either the leg or the shoulder**
- **1 onion, thinly sliced**
- **salt and pepper to taste**
- **juice of 1 lemon**
- **2 tbsp wine or cider**
- **6 small tomatoes**
- **6–10 button mushrooms**
- **small amount melted butter**
- **boiled rice, to serve**

You can buy lamb ready diced or, if you are shopping at a local butcher's shop, they will dice it for you. If you have bought a shoulder or leg joint, you should cut the lamb off the bone and trim off any fat. Cut the meat into 1-cm/½-in cubes. Put these into a bowl and scatter the onion slices over the top. Sprinkle over the salt, pepper, lemon juice and the wine or cider, cover and leave overnight in the fridge to marinate. Put the lamb cubes on to skewers, alternating them with the vegetables. Brush with a little melted butter. Grill/broil for 15 minutes, turning them frequently. These quantities should be sufficient for six people. You could reduce for two or freeze the kebabs.

Beef

Beef is available all year round, but can be expensive. Butchers and markets tend to have a wide variety of different cuts. They can also advise you on how to cook it. Grocery-store beef labels usually tell you how to prepare and cook the meat. Beef is rich in vitamin B, iron, zinc, phosphorous and selenium.

Choosing Beef

Avoid wet, slimy meat, and a marbled effect will indicate that there is a high fat content, which you may wish to avoid. Colour is not a great indicator, but if the beef is packed straight after slaughter then it will be bright red, and if it is brown then the meat has been open to the air for some time. Beef should be firm to the touch. You can also find naturally matured beef, which may be a burgundy colour, with a yellowish fat.

Roasting Beef

A joint from the back ribs, fillet or sirloin is ideal for roasting, if a little expensive. A 1.5 kg/3 lb 5 oz boned joint will feed six people. Preheat your oven to 190°C/375°F/Gas Mark 5. Then sear the joint by rolling it in a hot pan for 10 minutes and transfer the beef to your roasting tin and cook in the oven for the required time. Check the beef is cooked by using a meat thermometer. Timing guidelines are as follows:

Rare: To achieve rare beef, you need to cook it for 11 minutes per 450 g/1 lb and the thermometer should read 60°C/140°F.

Medium: This requires 14 minutes per 450 g/1 lb and the thermometer should read 70°C/160°F.

Well done: This requires 16 minutes per 450 g/1 lb and the thermometer should read 80°C/180°F.

Pot Roasting and Braising

For pot roasting and braising, choose brisket, thick flank, topside or silverside. Dust with flour; fry it to brown, then place the beef on vegetables and herbs in your pot. Cover the meat with stock and cook on a gentle heat in the oven, with a lid on. If you have cooked a joint of beef and you have some left over, let it cool and either freeze or refrigerate as soon as possible. Never put hot meat into the fridge.

Cheaper Cuts of Beef

Stewing, braising and casseroling are the best ways to tenderize less expensive cuts of beef. The cheaper cuts of meat usually require a longer and slower cooking time. You can also roast knuckle joint, blade and rib joints, as well as brisket and silverside. They are flavoursome and succulent. And again, of course, do not forget mince as another option. Cheaper cuts of beef to look out for include:

- chuck steak
- brisket
- shin
- neck
- blade
- flank
- knuckle joints

Beef Stew

This recipe will feed six people and would easily keep in the fridge for two days. You will need:

- 700 g/1½ lb stewing steak
- 2 large carrots
- 2 large turnips
- 1 large onion
- 900 ml/1½ pts/scant 1 qt water or stock

First, cut up the meat into cubes. You could ask your butcher to do this for you. Roll the meat in a little flour. Fry the meat until it is lightly browned. Slice up the vegetables into either cubes or strips. Fry the onion until it is lightly coloured. Put all of the ingredients into a large pot, add the water or stock and place over a gentle heat until it starts to boil. Add salt and pepper to taste. Cover the pan with a lid and gently simmer the stew for 2 to 2½ hours, until the meat is tender.

Poultry

Chicken, turkey, duck, goose and the more exotic quail are no longer seasonal birds but are available all year round, fresh or frozen. Intensively reared chicken is very cheap but they can lack flavour and can be watery, not to mention the ethical drawbacks. Free range or organic poultry may be more expensive, but with care you can produce two or three meals from a single whole bird.

Choosing Chicken

Chickens in your grocery store probably come with more variety than any other type of meat. Corn-fed chickens have a yellow flesh, capons are also fattened on corn and have more fat. You need to make sure that the chicken is well wrapped; it should be undamaged and the meat should be firm and plump. Fresh chicken will have a better flavour because frozen birds are not hung. If there is ice between the wrapper and the skin, this means that the chicken has thawed and been refrozen. Do not buy this from your store.

Choosing Cuts

It is nearly always proportionately cheaper to buy a whole bird than individual cuts. You can pay the same price for two breasts as you can for a whole chicken. A whole chicken will give you two thighs, two wings, two breasts, two drumsticks and the carcass from which you can make your own stock or soup (*see* pages 174–75 for tips on making stocks). Chicken legs or drumsticks are fattier than the breast meat. Thighs, which have darker meat, are also fattier but they do have a richer flavour. Chicken wings, whilst cheap, actually have very little meat but are fine for barbecuing.

Cooking a Whole Chicken

Heat the oven to 190°C/375°F/Gas Mark 5. Put the chicken into a roasting tin and loosely cover with kitchen foil. Cook for 20 minutes plus an additional 20 minutes for every 450 g/1 lb of weight. Take the foil off for the last 30 minutes of cooking to brown the skin. To check to see if the chicken is cooked, pierce the plumpest part of the chicken with a fork. The juices should run clear and not pink. To improve the taste, you can season the chicken with salt and pepper before roasting and you can place a whole, peeled onion inside the carcass. Do not forget that, if you have a big enough roasting tin, you could put your vegetables to roast around the chicken about an hour before it is cooked.

Vegetables

Vegetables that are harvested in their natural seasons and environment have a far better flavour and they are cheaper too, as they have not been grown out of season and flown halfway across the globe. Roasted root vegetables in winter are comforting and herby salads are wonderful in the summer. You do not need to buy organic, but you should watch out for particular vegetables that may have been irradiated, or otherwise treated to improve their shelf life.

Tips on Buying Vegetables

Try to buy your vegetables fresh and not in bulk as they will not last for many days.
If the vegetables look discoloured or wilted, then these have been on the shelves too long.
Look out for vegetables that have firm skins and unblemished flesh, and avoid those with
brown patches or bruised and pulpy flesh, or damp or musty smelling vegetables.

Preparing Vegetables

You can cook your vegetables in almost any way imaginable, but here are some tips on how
to prepare them:

 Wash them thoroughly: This will remove dirt and traces of pesticides.

 Only peel if necessary: Never peel too thickly, as many of the nutrients
are just below the skin.

Prepare to preserve: Why not prepare your vegetables to use, but freeze them
instead? Lay them out on a tray and freeze until they are solid and then transfer to
the freezer bag.

Steaming and Boiling

Steaming is a healthy way of cooking vegetables. They do not lose as many vitamins and
they keep their flavour and texture. Cut them into even sizes to make sure that they have the
same cooking time. You can boil vegetables; green vegetables should be boiled in salted water
to retain their colour. Be careful not to over-boil vegetables as they will become too soft and
lose more of their nutrients.

Other Ways of Cooking Vegetables

Stick to frying or stir-frying for soft vegetables like mushrooms, beans and onions. Oven
baking is ideal for root vegetables, squashes and sweet potatoes. Aubergines/eggplants

and courgettes/zucchini are delicious when grilled/broiled. You can puree squashes and root vegetables after you have cooked them; just add butter, milk and herbs to taste. Other vegetables can be stuffed, such as potatoes, aubergines, courgettes and tomatoes.

Roasted Courgettes/Zucchini with Garlic

This recipe is very simple and takes little preparation time. Use the courgettes as an accompaniment to slow-roasted lamb and take advantage of the oven being on. To prepare, top and tail six medium-sized courgettes, then make a small slit along the centre of each. Place the courgettes in a lightly oiled ovenproof dish and place a clove of garlic into the slit you have cut in each one. Grate a fresh tomato over the courgettes and season with salt and freshly ground pepper. Cover the ovenproof dish with kitchen foil and bake for 1 hour in the oven with any of your roast meat dishes.

Rice & Pasta

Rice and grains are diet staples across the world. They can provide the basis of a huge number of different dishes, from risottos to stews and from cakes to salads. They are economical, healthy and delicious. Pastas are essentially Italian, but they come in a huge variety of different types: spaghetti, macaroni and lasagne, to name just a few. Pasta can be fresh or dried and the hundreds of different pasta shapes allow sauces to cling on to them in different ways. More liquid sauces need thin and long pasta, thicker sauces are ideal with more complicated pasta shapes. The recipes at the end of this book include many rice, pasta or noodle options.

Varieties of Rice

There are lots of different rice types, many of which come in both white and brown/wholegrain varieties. The purplish, black wild rice is not, in fact, a rice but an aquatic grass and it is much more expensive as it is difficult to harvest. In addition to their colour, rice grains are long-, medium- or short-grain:

Long-grain: This rice will stay separate and fluffy if cooked properly. Examples include Basmati, Jasmine, American long-grain (such as Carolina) and others known simply as 'long-grain'.

 Medium-grain: This rice is often used in risottos or paellas. The category includes the Carnaroli risotto rice.

 Short-grain: This rice can be used in risottos, puddings or as sushi rice. It is more sticky. The Arborio risotto rice is a short-grain rice.

Preparing Rice and Grains

If you want your dish to be creamy, never wash your rice before you cook it. However, if you were making sushi, then you would need to wash the rice several times before cooking. Washing gets rid of some of the starch and gives you a fluffier rice. Wholegrain rice should be rinsed to minimize the froth when you boil the rice. Soaking grains can help reduce the cooking time, but it never makes a great deal of difference so may not be worth the effort.

Cooking Rice and Grains

Because there are so many different types of grain, it is difficult to be precise about the cooking times. Always follow the method on the packet. Measure out rice by volume and not by weight. As a side dish, you will need 65 g/2½ oz/⅓ cup of rice per person. Cook in double the amount of liquid. You only need to simmer in a covered saucepan for 15 minutes and then drain. Fluff up the rice with a fork before you serve it. You can use cold, cooked rice or grains in salads or soups, or stuff vegetables like aubergines/eggplants with it. Do not store cooked rice for more than a day, even in the fridge, as it can cause food poisoning.

Cooking Pasta

Whether you are cooking fresh or dried pasta, you will need a large pan of boiling water, with a pinch of salt and a drop of oil added. For every 450 g/1 lb pasta, you will need 6 l/10½ pts/25 cups water. The pasta should be completely submerged and you need to bring it up to the boil. The pasta is ready when it feels elastic but there is some resistance when you bite into it. Drain the pasta out using a colander. As a guide, use these quantities per person:

 dried pasta – 75–125 g/3–4 oz

fresh pasta – 125–150 g/4–5 oz

filled pasta – 175–200 g/6–7 oz

Noodles

Noodles are available dried, fresh or ready-cooked, again in a wide range of shapes and sizes. Egg noodles can be used in soups and stir-fries, rice noodles in soups or meat dishes and mung bean noodles as a noodle dish or in sauces. You can steam, stir-fry or deep-fry noodles. As a guide, use these quantities per person:

 dried noodles – 75–125 g/3–4 oz
 fresh noodles – 125–150 g/4–5 oz

One-pot Meals

The advantages of one-pot meals for beginners are that they use few items of cookware, the washing up is thus minimized, they are usually very simple to make and they are versatile – you can vary your ingredients and add them throughout the cooking time, adding extra vegetables or fresh herbs. Slow-cooked casserole-type dishes are one kind of one-pot meal; simmering food slowly is an ancient form of cooking. It gives the ingredients a chance to tenderize and blend and brings out the flavour. You need to be gentle because as soon as you put in any meat or fish, the mixture should not be allowed to boil, otherwise you might end up eating tough and rubbery chunks. One-pot meals do not necessarily take long to prepare or even cook, however.

Afelia

This very simple Greek recipe is an ideal one-pot casserole that serves four people (do not forget, you can always freeze leftovers!). You will need:

- 450 g/15 oz/2¼ cups diced pork
- 150 ml/5 fl oz/²⁄₃ cup red wine
- 2 tbsp olive or vegetable oil
- 1 tsp each of cardamom pods and coriander seeds
- fresh coriander/cilantro, to garnish
- salt and pepper, to season

Put the pork into a glass dish or bowl and cover with the red wine. Place in the fridge to marinate for at least 2 hours. Take the pork out of the marinade and dry it with a paper towel. Brown the pork in a saucepan with a little of the oil, then put it to one side. Put the remainder of the oil into the saucepan and gently cook the cardamom pods and coriander seeds until you can smell them strongly. Pour the wine marinade over the spices and then add the pork. Season to taste. Bring the pot to a boil and then reduce to a simmer and cook for 40 minutes. You will know when the meat is cooked, as the liquid will have been reduced and thickened. Serve on a bed of rice.

Following Recipes

Cooking is all about personal taste and recipes are just guidelines for the techniques and ideas. If you are new to cooking, then make sure that you read the recipe carefully – all the way through – before you start because some steps may need to be taken before others. Parts of the recipe may require preparation. You can weigh and measure everything out in advance and have them ready to be added as and when they are needed. The recipe book will be your bible to start with. You will find, though, that the more times you cook a dish, the more confident you will get about tweaking it slightly to experiment. Seasoning and adding herbs is a matter of personal taste and can easily be adjusted.

Cooking for Fewer People

There are different ways of approaching a recipe that is designed for more people than you are cooking for:

 Reduce quantities: A recipe for four when there are only two of you requires you to reduce all the main ingredients by half, or down to a third if the recipe was designed for six people, for example.

 Cook the full quantity: Cook the recipe for four – this will give you a ready-made meal that only needs to be reheated, either from the freezer or the fridge.

 Use leftover elements in other meals: If you are cooking joints of meat or whole poultry and there is plenty left over, then these can provide the basis for a variety of other meals later in the week, as we will discover in the next part of this chapter.

Make Your Own

Not only is it possible to make your own delicious meals from scratch, cheaply and easily, you can also go one step further and make your own bread, cakes, pastry and even pasta from scratch. By buying the raw ingredients rather than the finished product, you can get much more for your money and learn some invaluable skills at the same time! And it is always good to know exactly what has (or has not) gone into the food you eat.

Bake Your Own Bread

Bread machines have tumbled in price, but there is nothing quite like hand baking. You can really work out all your frustrations and tensions on that dough. Even better, it is cheaper and such a triumph when you pull your loaf or rolls out of the oven and take in that unbeatable fresh baked aroma. There is nothing like working the dough and making your own home-made loaf. You know what has gone into it and you will be rewarded for your time and effort, because you have made something really special.

Flour

The best flours to use are the ones described as strong or very strong. It is actually the protein content that forms the gluten that is so important in baking. The higher the protein level, the more gluten and this gives your loaf an excellent crumb structure. These types of flour also absorb more liquid, which gives them wonderful consistency and texture. They will also give your loaf volume and colour. Although you can experiment by mixing different types of flour, avoid self-raising and plain flour because they do not have enough protein for bread. Here are your options:

☑ **Strong or very strong white**: Ideal for classic white bread.

☑ **Strong or very strong wholemeal**: For bread with rich flavour and texture.

☑ **Strong brown**: Produces a traditional wholemeal loaf with a lighter texture. Try mixing half strong white and half strong wholemeal for a light, nutty wholemeal loaf.

☑ **Multigrain**: This can give your loaf a unique texture and flavour, as there are seeds and grains added to the mix.

Storing the Flour

Your flour should never get damp, so store it in a cool dry place in a sealed container. You can store your flour in the freezer, but you need to make sure it thaws out and comes up to room temperature before you use it. White flour will last longer than wholemeal flour because it has a higher fat content. Raising agents in self-raising flour will begin to lose their effectiveness once the sell-by date has passed. So do not be tempted to use old flour.

A Basic Loaf by Hand

There is nothing wrong with using dried yeast, so all you will need for a basic loaf is:

- 650 g/1 lb 5 oz/5 cups strong white flour
- 1 tsp salt
- 1 tsp sugar
- 1 sachet easy-bake yeast
- 1 tbsp vegetable oil
- 400 ml/14 fl oz/1^2/$_3$ cups warm water

Follow this easy method. Put the flour, salt and sugar into a warm bowl and stir in the yeast. Then add the oil and water and mix to a soft dough. Turn out the mix on to a floured surface and knead for 10 minutes. Then shape and put into a greased tin. Leave to prove until it has doubled in size – this could take 1^1/$_2$–2 hours. Place in an oven preheated to 220°C/425°F/Gas Mark 7, then turn the heat down to 200°C/400°F/Gas Mark 6 immediately. Bake for 25 to 30 minutes. Turn out the loaf on to a wire tray to cool. You will know if the loaf is cooked if you tap the bottom of the loaf and it sounds hollow.

Mixing and Kneading

Make sure that the mixing bowl is warm. Once you have mixed the ingredients, you will need to make sure that the dough is kneaded thoroughly. By kneading the dough, you will be strengthening the gluten. Put the dough out on to a floured surface and fold it towards you. Push down on the dough, pushing it away from you with the base of your hand. Turn the

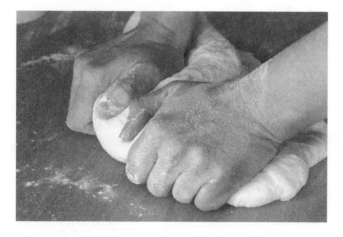

dough 90° and repeat the 'fold and push'. Keep doing this until the dough feels smooth and elastic.

Proving, Knocking Back and Proving Again

After you have kneaded the dough, you can put it into a bowl and cover it with clingfilm. This stops a skin from forming on the dough. Put the dough in a warm place and wait for it to double in size. An airing cupboard is ideal. With some loaves, you then need to knock back the dough by kneading it again for 2–3 minutes. This takes out the big air pockets. Let it double in size again and then bake it in the hot oven. If you are using easy-bake yeast, then you do not need to knock back.

Bread Makers

Your bread maker should come with a range of bread recipes. These tell you exactly the order in which to add the ingredients and the amounts you will need. The only major problems with bread makers are:

 Imperfect bottoms: At the bottom of the bread tin, there is a paddle that mixes the dough. This always makes it difficult to get the loaf out without damaging it.

 Sticky tins: If you have not greased the bread tin thoroughly, then the loaf will often stick.

 Unappealing shapes: You might not like the shape of the loaf, as bread machines tend to make boxy-looking loaves.

Bake Your Own Cakes

Baking your own cakes should hold no terrors. Here are some general points and handy hints to remember:

 Preheat: Nearly all of the recipes need a ready-heated oven.

 The right pans: Shiny metal pans produce the best cakes. Dark pans absorb heat and cakes baked in these usually need the oven to be set slightly lower than the recipe.

Avoid sticking: Unless the recipe says otherwise, always grease and flour pans.

Ingredients' temperature: Always use eggs and butter or margarine at room temperature and not straight from the fridge.

Positioning: Always bake on a centre rack in the oven.

When is it done?: Test cakes to see if they are done by using a toothpick. If the toothpick comes out with a few dry crumbs and no wet cake mixture, the cake is ready.

Cooling off period: Always allow your cake 10 minutes to cool on a wire rack. And let cakes cool before you ice/frost them, otherwise the icing might melt!

Slicing layers: Use a serrated knife to trim cake layers so they will sit evenly.

Freezing: If you want to freeze your cakes, do not frost them. Cakes will last six months in the freezer if frozen fresh.

A Basic Cake

There are literally thousands of cake recipes, but the most versatile basic cake recipe needs the following ingredients:

- 175g/6 oz/³⁄₄ cup soft margarine
- 175g/6 oz/⁷⁄₈ cup caster/superfine sugar
- 175g/6 oz/1¹⁄₃ cups self-raising flour
- 3 eggs
- 1 tsp baking powder

Heat the oven to 170°C/325°F/Gas Mark 3. Then mix all the ingredients together in a bowl until evenly mixed. Spoon the ingredients into a greased and lined 18-cm/7-in round cake tin and bake for 55 minutes. Leave to cool before turning out on to a cooling rack. Sprinkle the top with icing/confectioner's sugar or spread your favourite jam on top before serving.

Tomato Soup Cake

This may sound pretty odd but it is a cheap and fun way of adding a great rich, moist, spicy quality to your cake. People will never know what the main ingredient is! You will need:

- 250 g/9 oz/2 cups flour
- 4 tsp baking powder
- 1 tsp bicarbonate of soda/baking soda
- 250 g/9 oz/1⅓ cup sugar
- 1 tsp cinnamon
- ½ tsp ground cloves
- 1½ tsp allspice
- 300 g/10 oz can tomato soup
- ½ cup vegetable oil
- 120ml/4 fl oz/½ cup milk or water
- 2 eggs

Mix all of the dry ingredients together in a large bowl. Then add all of the wet ingredients. Combine them and then pour them into a 33 cm/13 in x 23 cm/9 in baking tin that you have greased. Put into an oven preheated to 180°C/350°F/Gas Mark 4. Bake for 40 minutes, cool on a wire rack and cover with cream cheese frosting.

Making Your Cream Cheese Frosting

You can make this frosting quite quickly. Ideally, put all of the ingredients below into a food processor and blend until smooth, although you can do this by hand with a whisk.

- 125 g/4 oz/½ cup cream cheese or mascarpone cheese
- 250 g/9 oz/1¼ cups icing/confectioner's sugar
- 90 g/3½ oz/⅓ cup unsalted butter
- ½ tsp vanilla essence/extract
- juice of half a lemon

Bake Your Own Pies

Home-made pie crusts are so much better than store-bought varieties. Think of the sense of achievement and the money you will save. And pie-making could not be easier. All you need is four basic ingredients for the pie crust:

 Flour: To form the structure and the bulk.

 Fat: To add flavour and create texture.

✓ **Liquid**: To bind the dough.

✓ **Salt**: To add flavour and help brown the crust.

Shortcrust Pastry

This is ideal for pies and tarts. You will need:

- 225 g/8 oz/1³⁄₄ cups plain/all-purpose flour
- pinch salt
- 115 g/4 oz/¹⁄₂ cup butter or margarine
- cold water, to mix

Sift the flour and salt together. Rub in the butter or margarine, then mix to a stiff paste by adding the cold water. Roll and shape the dough to fit your pie dish. Glaze the top with beaten egg before cooking.

Flaky Pastry

This pastry is ideal for pies, tarts and tartlets. You will need:

- 450 g/1 lb/3¹⁄₂ cups plain/all-purpose flour
- pinch salt
- 275 g/10 oz/1¹⁄₄ cups butter or margarine
- cold water, to mix
- ¹⁄₂ tsp lemon juice

Sift the flour and salt. Divide the butter or margarine into 4 portions. Rub a quarter into the flour. Mix to a soft dough with the water and lemon juice. Roll out the pastry and place another quarter of the butter on the top of the pastry. Fold the pastry up and press the edges together with a rolling pin. Repeat the process with the two remaining butter or margarine portions. Glaze the top of your pie with beaten egg or milk. Always put the flaky pastry into a hot oven preheated to 190°F/375°F/Gas Mark 5.

Puff Pastry

This pastry is good for pies, tarts, vol-au-vents and patties. You will need:

- 450 g/1 lb/3½ cups plain/all-purpose flour
- pinch salt
- 450 g/1 lb/2 cups butter or margarine
- cold water, to mix
- ½ tsp lemon juice

Sift together the flour and salt, then add the lemon juice and water to mix to a smoothish dough. Knead the dough well and roll it into a strip. Place about an eighth of the butter on to the rolled out pastry and fold in half. Press the edges of the dough down with a rolling pin. Repeat this process until all the butter or margarine has been used. Leave the pastry to cool before shaping in your pie dish. Glaze with beaten egg, then bake in a very hot oven (230°C/450°F/Gas Mark 8).

Sweet Pastry

Sweet pastry is perfect when you are making desserts, such as fruit pies, mince pies or jam tarts. You will need:

- 450 g/1 lb/3¹⁄₂ cups plain/all-purpose flour
- pinch salt
- 150 g/5 oz/²⁄₃ cup butter or margarine
- cold water, to mix, if required
- rind of ¹⁄₂ a lemon, finely grated
- 225 g/8 oz/1 heaped cup caster/superfine sugar
- 1 egg

Sift the flour and salt. Rub in the butter and add the caster sugar and the lemon rind. Mix to a stiff dough with the beaten egg and cold water if necessary. Roll out as you would shortcrust pastry and line your pie dish. Add your filling and glaze the top of the pie with beaten egg or milk.

Hints for Pastry Making

Cool: Keep everything cool and, if possible, work on a cool surface.

Sift: Always sift the flour.

Rub it in: When you use your fingers to rub in the butter or margarine, lift up your hands so the air is caught.

Go easy on the water: Do not use too much water or the pastry will be hard.

Lighter with lemons: Lemon juice makes the pastry lighter.

Speed and technique: Work quickly and do not over-handle the pastry. Roll the pastry lightly, quickly and evenly, with short strokes. Always roll away from you and not from side to side.

 Rest: Allow the pastry to stand for a short time after you have made it. Allow 15 minutes for the pastry to relax between each rolling when making puff or flaky pastry.

 Take sides: Use the rolled side of the pastry for the outside.

 Turn up the heat: You need a fairly hot oven – the richer the pastry, the hotter the oven will need to be, as it will make the pastry lighter.

General Baking Tips

Freezing Cakes and Pies

Always allow items that you are intending to freeze to cool down completely. And one of the big problems with cakes and pies is that the temptation is to freeze them in the dish in which

you baked them. A great way round this is to buy disposable foil dishes or cake tins. These can go straight into the freezer. Smaller cakes can easily be frozen in plastic containers or even in freezer bags. If you are worried they will get squashed, then freeze them individually on a flat tray and then put them into their freezer-friendly container.

Batch-baking Cakes and Pies

If you are going to be making your own cakes and pies, why not fill your freezer with them and double, treble and even quadruple your ingredients? If you have found a pie filling that was too great a bargain to ignore, then it makes sense to make several pies at the same time. Work it like a production line: make your pastry, prepare your fillings, line your dishes, insert your fillings, place your pie crust on top of each, then bake together – your oven will probably fit 3 or 4 requiring the same temperature at the same time.

Make Your Own Pasta

You can find an enormous selection of dried and fresh pasta in the grocery stores. Some of it is really good and you can vary a meal by trying out different sauces. But how much better would it be to make your own? You might need to invest in a pasta making machine but you could save money in the long run. The best ones are the hand-cranked versions. They give you more control. You can add different ingredients, like spinach or even octopus ink, to the basic mixture to give you colour and variety. See page 189 for a great recipe using home-made pasta; and see also the recipe on page 190 for making your own gnocchi!

How to Make Pasta

You will need:

- 300 g/10 oz/2⅓ cups pasta flour
- 2 large/extra-large eggs
- some lukewarm water

Put the flour on your work surface and make a hole in the middle ready for the eggs. Beat the eggs and mix in with the flour to create a smooth dough. Knead the mixture with the palm of your hand. If the mixture gets too crumbly, add some water. You are looking for a smooth and silky texture for the dough. Once you have this, roll the dough up into a ball and leave it to rest in a covered bowl for around 20 minutes.

The Pasta Machine

If you have a pasta machine, it does make life simpler for making certain shapes, mainly ribbon pasta:

 Passing through: Pass the dough through the rollers of the pasta machine several times to make a thin sheet of pasta. Each time you pass it through, dust it with flour to stop it sticking. You will need to do this 6–8 times, by which point the dough will be soft and elastic. You can reduce the space between the rollers each time; do this one notch at a time. If the sheet gets too big to handle, cut it in half.

 Cutting into shape: Once made, leave the sheet or sheets for ten minutes before passing through the cutter (if making ribbon pasta).

 Use now or later: You can use the pasta right away or you can dry it or freeze it for later use. To dry, simply hang the strands and then store in an airtight container.

Stretching Food

If you have more mouths to feed or you simply want to make your food go further, then you need to focus on the cheapest ingredient in the meal. Beans, canned tomatoes, potatoes or vegetables that are in season, dried pasta, rice and grains are all ideal choices of how to stretch food a little further without stretching your budget. We have seen that you can take advantage of special offers or deals in the grocery store by stocking up in bulk when basic staples are available and now is your chance to use them.

Making Food Go Further

You can use fruit and cereals to make dishes go further. You could also use smaller baking dishes and, rather than make one large pie, you could make two smaller ones. You could drop raisins into chillies, rice and bean dishes or stews – in a chilli, you could add a whole cup of raisins. This will give you extra but it will also change the texture and give sweetness to the dish. If you serve the chilli on rice or with bread, it is an extremely inexpensive meal. If your chilli or stew is too thin, you could add half a cup of cornflakes or uncooked oatmeal. This will thicken the liquid but also stretch the dish.

Stretching Pies

If you are going to bake a pie, why not bake two instead of one, with the same amount of ingredients? Just use two shallower pie tins instead of one deeper tin. Put one of the pies into the freezer. You can also slice the pies up in advance into slightly smaller, individual servings. Freeze each portion separately and use them as you need them, rather than over-filling a plate.

Excess Water

You can even save the water from cooked pasta or beans. Pour it off into a jar and put it into the fridge. You can add it to dishes in the future and it will form the basis of a broth or a stock. The water will retain the taste of the pasta or beans and will add a better flavour to the dish you are now cooking than plain water.

Making Meals with Few Ingredients

You do not need an enormous number of ingredients to produce a tasty and satisfying meal for two. Think about two vegetables and one meat ingredient and there are literally hundreds of combinations. Onions and leeks make dishes tasty and bulkier and allow you to stretch the size of what is on your plate. Two or three handfuls of dried pasta and one small tin of own-brand tuna will provide each person with a filling meal. One chicken breast, some chicken stock, a pack of rice noodles, a chopped garlic clove and 2 teaspoons soy sauce will give you chicken noodle soup in less than 20 minutes.

Using Leftovers

Here are some basic ideas, before you even consider freezing any leftovers:

- **Stale bread and rolls**: Do not throw these out, use them for breadcrumbs or croutons to serve with fruit, salad and soups. You can also use stale bread for bread and butter pudding.

✅ **Cooked fish**: This can be crumbled or flaked over a salad with a little oil for dressing.

✅ **Cooked vegetables**: Veggies can be turned into a salad by adding chopped onion, mayonnaise, lettuce and some dried herbs. Or puree them to form the basis of a soup.

✅ **Scraps of meat**: Cooked chicken and beef scraps, for example, can be combined with mayonnaise or creamed cheese, or partnered with chutneys and pickles, to make sandwich fillings – turkey sandwiches are not just for Christmas! They can also be used in soups. Some of the recipes in the following chapters use ready-cooked chicken and meat in a variety of ways.

Roast Dinner Soup

Instead of cooking a roast dinner for two, cook enough vegetables for four (including parsnips). The following day, all you will need for your soup is:

✅ **the cooked roast vegetables**
✅ **any other cooked vegetables you might not have eaten**
✅ **enough meat stock to cover the vegetables in a pan**
✅ **some ground black pepper**
✅ **croutons and a little grated cheese**

Combine the vegetables, stock and pepper in a saucepan. Bring to the boil and simmer for 10 minutes. Then liquidize the soup or use a hand blender to pulp the vegetables. Serve with grated cheese and toasted croutons.

Bubble and Squeak Cakes

If you have vegetables left after a roast dinner, no need to worry. Use them in that old favourite, Bubble and Squeak! You will need:

- 1 red onion, finely chopped
- 4 rashers streaky bacon
- leftover mixed cooked vegetables, chopped into small pieces
- leftover mashed potato
- 25 g/1 oz/¼ cup each grated cheese and butter
- salt and pepper, to taste

Gently fry the onion for 4–5 minutes until soft. Cut the bacon into strips and cook for 4 minutes until golden brown. Transfer the bacon and onions to a large bowl and add the leftover vegetables and mashed potato and season with salt and pepper. Add the cheese, then, using your hands, shape each portion into a cake. Put a little flour on a plate and coat each cake with it on both sides. Grease a baking tray with the butter. Put the cakes on to the tray and bake for 25 minutes at 200°C/400°F/Gas Mark 8. This is a delicious accompaniment to sliced cold meat if you have any left over from your roast dinner. Bubble and squeak cakes freeze brilliantly.

Cooking Too Much and Freezing

Some people cook once a month. They cook enough meals to last them and freeze everything, ready to fit in with their busy lives. You do nt have to bulk cook to take advantage of the freezer, but every time you make a lasagne, why not make two? Curries, vegetable soup, loaves of home-baked bread, pies, pasties, meatballs, quiches, bolognese sauce, cottage pies, chilli con carne and other mince dishes are all ideal to prepare in advance and freeze. You can make several pizza bases and freeze them. Cakes – again, make two and freeze one. You can always freeze biscuit dough and pastry too. It is a great way to use up your bargain bulk staples, or to make sure you make the best use of fruit and vegetables when they are in season and at their cheapest. Other ideas for great things to put in the freezer are:

- **pasta sauces**
- **apple puree**
- **toppings for fruit crumbles**
- **portions of blanched vegetables**
- **sliced, home-cooked meats**
- **sliced, cooked hams**
- **vegetables you have grown yourself and have not cooked yet**
- **home-made, cooked mince pies**
- **home-made, cooked sausage rolls**

A Few Words on Containers

Ideally, whatever you use to package up your food for the freezer, it needs to be:

- **Odourless, tasteless and greaseproof**: You do not want your food to take on the smell or taste of a whiffy plastic container.

- **Moisture- and vapour-proof**: The food must remain in good condition and this means not getting ice on it through air and moisture seeping in.

- **Leak-proof**: This is especially important if the contents are very liquid – they will not freeze immediately!

Tough and durable: They must be resistant to becoming brittle and cracking at low temperatures so they do not split in the freezer.

 Easy to seal and label: This is important for identification purposes – you will never remember when you put something in the freezer and some items are not easy to pick out of a line-up when frozen!

 Preferably reusable: This will cut down on costs – a cook on a budget will freeze lots.

 Designed to stack or pack: You need to make maximum use of space for all the food you will be freezing.

 Reasonably priced: This may seem obvious but it is worth stating – otherwise your efforts will not have paid off.

Avoiding Wastage

Even if you shop weekly, your fridge will probably look fairly sad a day or two before you go shopping again. This is the most tempting time to buy a takeaway or eat a ready meal from the freezer. But think before you do this – you can undoubtedly squeeze more out of your fridge than you realize. All you might need is a portion of butter, milk or a couple of eggs as the key ingredient to make use of leftover bits and pieces in the fridge. Eggs, for instance, are a great basis for omelettes, even if you just add fried rice or some dried herbs.

Make a Spanish Omelette

Your Spanish omelette can contain whatever you wish. There is no hard and fast rule about the ingredients – carrots, potatoes, onions, courgettes/zucchini, tomatoes and all sorts of ingredients can all be used up rather than being wasted. What you will need is:

- leftover vegetables, chopped
- oil for cooking
- seasoning to taste (such as salt, pepper, herbs and/or spices)
- 4–6 eggs are enough for an omelette for two people
- grated cheese

Season and fry the leftover vegetables in a little oil until they are golden and will have warmed through. Beat the eggs and pour over the cooking vegetables. Swirl the frying pan so that the omelette mix is evenly distributed around the pan. When you can see that the omelette is becoming more solid, remove it from the hob. Sprinkle the cheese on top of the omelette and place it under a preheated hot grill/broiler. The cheese will melt and turn the top of the omelette a golden brown. Cut the omelette into portions and transfer to the serving plate. Serve with salad and crusty bread.

Home-made Stock

In order to make a good soup, you need to make good stock. This is where the carcass from Sunday's roast chicken comes in handy! You will need to add herbs, such as parsley, thyme and bay leaves. As well as chicken carcasses, you can also use:

- fresh vegetable trimmings
- meat bones
- inexpensive cuts of meat
- shells from shellfish

Do not use broccoli or cabbage as part of the stock, as they can be bitter and overwhelm the flavour. Also avoid using onion skins and brightly coloured ingredients, like beetroot.

Making the Stock

To add depth of flavour, you could sauté the ingredients or roast them before dropping them into an equal amount of cold water. Bring them to the boil and then simmer: a vegetable stock will take between 30 minutes and an hour, but a meat-based stock can take between 1 and 5 hours. Skim off the foam that appears on the surface of the stock and strain, using a sieve, as soon as possible after cooking.

Using the Stock

You can now use the stock to make soups or as a base for your gravy. To thicken the stock, use cornflour/cornstarch, rice, bulgur wheat, breadcrumbs, egg yolks, milk or yoghurt. To stop it from curdling or forming lumps, add your thickeners to a ladleful of the soup in a bowl. Mix well and then pour the mixture back into the soup pot. Serve your soup with crusty bread, croutons or even fritters and savoury biscuits. For an Asian-style soup, serve with rice.

Keeping the Stock

You can freeze stock or keep it in the refrigerator. But if you are intending to keep it for any length of time, it is best to freeze it as soon as it is cool. If you want small portions of the stock, say for gravies, you can pour the stock into ice cube trays or small baking tins. Let the stock freeze and then transfer the blocks into a freezer bag. Do not be tempted to pour your stock straight into a freezer bag: the likelihood is that it will spring a leak. You can always reduce your stock by continuing to let it simmer and then add extra water when you use it. That means it would take up less space in the freezer. Freezing the different flavoured stocks means you will always have one of the most important ingredients for soups ready to reheat.

Recipes:
Soups &
Starters

PACKED WITH
MONEY
SAVING
IDEAS & TIPS

Chinese Chicken Soup

Ingredients (Serves 4)

225 g/8 oz cooked chicken
1 tsp oil
6 spring onions/scallions, trimmed and
    diagonally sliced
1 red chilli, deseeded and finely chopped
1 garlic clove, peeled and crushed
2.5 cm/1 inch piece root ginger, peeled and
    finely grated
1 l/1¾ pts/1 qt chicken stock
150 g/5 oz/1½ cups medium egg noodles
1 carrot, peeled and cut into matchsticks
125 g/¾ cups bean sprouts
2 tbsp soy sauce
1 tbsp fish sauce
fresh coriander/cilantro leaves, to garnish

Remove any skin from the chicken. Place on a chopping/cutting board and use two forks to tear the chicken into fine shreds.

Heat the oil in a large saucepan and fry the spring onions and chilli for 1 minute.

Add the garlic and ginger and cook for another minute.

Stir in the chicken stock and gradually bring the mixture to the boil.

Break up the noodles a little and add to the boiling stock with the carrot.

Stir to mix, then reduce the heat to a simmer and cook for 3–4 minutes.

Add the shredded chicken, bean sprouts, soy sauce and fish sauce and stir.

Cook for a further 2–3 minutes until piping hot. Ladle the soup into bowls and sprinkle with the coriander leaves. Serve immediately.

Budget Tip
Since this recipe uses cooked chicken, it is a great way to use leftover chicken from that roast dinner.

Curried Parsnip Soup

Ingredients (Serves 4)

1 tsp cumin seeds
2 tsp coriander seeds
1 tsp oil
1 onion, peeled and chopped
1 garlic clove, peeled and crushed
1/2 tsp turmeric
1/4 tsp chilli powder
1 cinnamon stick
450 g/1 lb/2 cups parsnips, peeled and chopped
1 l/1¾ pts/1 qt vegetable stock
salt and freshly ground black pepper
2–3 tbsp low-fat natural/plain yoghurt, to serve
fresh coriander/cilantro leaves, to garnish

 In a small frying pan, dry-fry the cumin and coriander seeds over a moderately high heat for 1–2 minutes. Shake the pan during cooking until the seeds are lightly toasted.

Reserve until cooled. Grind the toasted seeds in a pestle and mortar.

Heat the oil in a saucepan. Cook the onion until softened and starting to turn golden.

Add the garlic, turmeric, chilli powder and cinnamon stick to the pan. Continue to cook for a further minute.

 Add the parsnips and stir well.

 Pour in the stock and bring to the boil. Cover and simmer for 4 minutes or until the parsnips are cooked.

Allow the soup to cool. Once cooled, remove the cinnamon stick and discard.

Blend the soup in a food processor until very smooth.

 Transfer to a saucepan and reheat gently. Season to taste with salt and pepper. Garnish with fresh coriander and serve immediately with the yoghurt.

Bread and Tomato Soup

Ingredients (Serves 4)

6 medium very ripe tomatoes
4 tbsp olive oil
1 onion, peeled and finely chopped
1 tbsp freshly chopped basil
3 garlic cloves, peeled and crushed
¼ tsp hot chilli powder
salt and freshly ground black pepper
600 ml/1 pt/2½ cups chicken stock
6 slices stale white bread
¼ small cucumber, cut into small dice
4 whole basil leaves

Make a small cross in the base of each tomato, then place in a bowl and cover with boiling water. Allow to stand for 2 minutes, or until the skins have started to peel away, then drain, remove the skins and seeds and chop into large pieces.

Heat 3 tablespoons of the olive oil in a saucepan and gently cook the onion until softened. Add the skinned tomatoes, chopped basil, garlic and chilli powder and season to taste with salt and pepper. Pour in the stock, cover the saucepan, bring to the boil and simmer gently for 15–20 minutes.

Remove the crusts from the bread and break into small pieces. Remove the tomato mixture from the heat and stir in the bread. Cover and leave to stand for 10 minutes, or until the bread has blended with the tomatoes. Season to taste. Serve warm or cold with a swirl of olive oil on the top, garnished with a spoonful of chopped cucumber and basil leaves.

Tasty Tip

This soup is best made when fresh tomatoes are in season. If you want to make it at other times of the year, replace the fresh tomatoes with 2 x 400 g/14 oz cans of peeled plum tomatoes. You may need to cook the soup for 5–10 minutes longer.

Lettuce Soup

Ingredients (Serves 4)

2 iceberg lettuces, quartered with hard
   core removed
1 tbsp olive oil
50 g/¹/₂ stick butter
125 g/¹/₂ cup spring onions/scallions,
   trimmed and chopped
1 tbsp freshly chopped parsley
1 tbsp plain/all-purpose flour
600 ml/1 pt/2¹/₂ cups chicken stock
salt and freshly ground black pepper
150 ml/¹/₄ pt/²/₃ cup single/light cream
¹/₄ tsp cayenne pepper, to taste
thick slices of stale ciabatta bread
sprig of parsley, to garnish

 Bring a large saucepan of water to the boil and blanch the lettuce leaves for 3 minutes. Drain and dry thoroughly on absorbent kitchen paper, then shred with a sharp knife.

Heat the oil and butter in a clean saucepan and add the lettuce, spring onions and parsley and cook together for 3–4 minutes, or until very soft.

Stir in the flour and cook for 1 minute, then gradually pour in the stock, stirring throughout. Bring to the boil and season to taste with salt and pepper. Reduce the heat, cover and simmer gently for 10–15 minutes.

 Allow the soup to cool slightly, then either sieve or puree in a blender. Alternatively, leave the soup chunky Stir in the cream, add more seasoning, to taste, if liked, then add the cayenne pepper.

Arrange the slices of ciabatta bread in a large soup dish or in individual bowls and pour the soup over the bread. Garnish with sprigs of parsley and serve immediately.

Helpful Hint

Do not prepare the lettuce too far in advance. Iceberg lettuce has a tendency to discolour when sliced, which may in turn discolour the soup.

Pasta and Bean Soup

Ingredients (Serves 4-6)

3 tbsp olive oil
2 celery stalks, trimmed and finely chopped
100 g/³⁄₄ cup prosciutto or prosciutto di speck,
   cut into pieces
1 red chilli, deseeded and finely chopped
2 large potatoes, peeled and cut into 2.5 cm/1 in cubes
2 garlic cloves, peeled and finely chopped
3 ripe plum tomatoes, skinned and chopped
1 x 400 g/14 oz can borlotti/cranberry beans, drained
   and rinsed
1 l/1³⁄₄ pts/1 qt chicken or vegetable stock
100 g/1 cup pasta shapes
large handful basil leaves, torn
salt and freshly ground black pepper
shredded basil leaves, to garnish
crusty bread, to serve

 Heat the olive oil in a heavy-based pan, add the celery and prosciutto and cook gently for 6–8 minutes, or until softened. Add the chopped chilli and potato cubes and cook for a further 10 minutes.

 Add the garlic to the chilli and potato mixture and cook for 1 minute. Add the chopped tomatoes and simmer for 5 minutes. Stir in two-thirds of the beans, then pour in the chicken or vegetable stock and bring to the boil.

 Add the pasta shapes to the soup stock and return it to simmering point. Cook the pasta for about 10 minutes, or until *al dente*.

 Meanwhile, place the remaining beans in a food processor or blender and blend with enough of the soup stock to make a smooth, thinnish puree.

 When the pasta is cooked, stir in the pureed beans with the torn basil. Season the soup to taste with salt and pepper. Ladle into serving bowls, garnish with shredded basil and serve immediately with plenty of crusty bread.

Helpful Hint

Other canned beans may be used if preferred. Try pinto beans, a smaller, paler version of the borlotti bean, or cannellini beans, which have a soft, creamy texture.

Cullen Skink

Ingredients (Serves 4)

25 g/1 oz/¼ stick unsalted butter
1 onion, peeled and chopped
1 fresh bay leaf
25 g/1 oz/3 tbsp plain/all-purpose flour
350 g/12 oz/3 cups new potatoes, scrubbed and
    cut into small pieces
600 ml/1 pt/2½ cups semi-skimmed/reduced-
    fat milk
300 ml/½ pt/1¼ cups water
350 g/12 oz undyed smoked haddock fillet, skinned
75 g/3 oz/½ cup sweetcorn kernels
50 g/2 oz/⅓ cup garden peas
freshly ground black pepper
½ tsp freshly grated nutmeg
2–3 tbsp single/light cream
2 tbsp freshly chopped parsley
crusty bread, to serve

Melt the butter in a large, heavy-based saucepan, add the onion and sauté for 3 minutes, stirring

occasionally. Add the bay leaf and stir, then sprinkle in the flour and cook over a low heat for 2 minutes, stirring frequently. Add the potatoes.

Take off the heat and gradually stir in the milk and water. Return to the heat and bring to the boil, stirring. Reduce the heat to a simmer and cook for 10 minutes.

Meanwhile, discard any pin bones from the fish and cut into small pieces. Add to the pan together with the sweetcorn and peas. Cover and cook gently, stirring occasionally, for 10 minutes, or until the vegetables and fish are cooked.

Add pepper and nutmeg to taste, then stir in the cream and heat gently for 1–2 minutes, or until piping hot. Sprinkle with the parsley and serve with crusty bread.

Helpful Hint
This recipe is great for beginners or those with little equipment, as it can all be made in one pot.

Tuna Chowder

Ingredients (Serves 4)

2 tsp oil
1 onion, peeled and finely chopped
2 sticks of celery, trimmed and finely sliced
1 tbsp plain/all-purpose flour
600 ml/1 pt/2½ cups skimmed milk
200 g/7 oz can tuna in water
325 g/11 oz can sweetcorn in water, drained
2 tsp freshly chopped thyme
salt and freshly ground black pepper
pinch cayenne pepper
2 tbsp freshly chopped parsley

Heat the oil in a large, heavy-based saucepan. Add the onion and celery and gently cook for about 5 minutes, stirring from time to time until the onion is softened.

Stir in the flour and cook for about 1 minute to thicken.

Draw the pan off the heat and gradually pour in the milk, stirring throughout.

Add the tuna and its liquid, the drained sweetcorn and the thyme.

Mix gently, then bring to the boil. Cover and simmer for 5 minutes.

Remove the pan from the heat and season to taste with salt and pepper.

Sprinkle the chowder with the cayenne pepper and chopped parsley. Divide into soup bowls and serve immediately.

Budget Tip
Using canned ingredients in your meals is a great way of cutting costs without losing much (if any) nutrition – and it is convenient too. This creamy soup also works well using equivalent amounts of canned crab meat instead of the tuna.

Cawl

Ingredients (Serves 4)

700 g/1½ lb scrag end of lamb or best
    end of neck chops
pinch of salt
2 large onions, peeled and thinly sliced
3 large potatoes, peeled and cut into chunks
2 parsnips, peeled and cut into chunks
1 swede/rutabaga peeled and cut into chunks
3 large carrots, peeled and cut into chunks
2 leeks, trimmed and sliced
freshly ground black pepper
4 tbsp freshly chopped parsley
warm crusty bread, to serve

☑ Put the lamb in a large saucepan, cover with cold water and bring to the boil. Add a generous pinch of salt. Simmer gently for 1½ hours, then set aside to cool completely, preferably overnight.

☑ The next day, skim the fat off the surface of the lamb liquid and discard.

☑ Return the saucepan to the heat and bring back to the boil. Simmer for 5 minutes. Add the onions, potatoes, parsnips, swede and carrots and return to the boil. Reduce the heat, cover and cook for about 20 minutes, stirring occasionally.

☑ Add the leeks and season to taste with salt and pepper. Cook for a further 10 minutes, or until all the vegetables are tender.

☑ Using a slotted spoon, remove the meat from the saucepan and take the meat off the bone. Discard the bones and any gristle, then return the meat to the pan. Adjust the seasoning to taste, stir in the parsley, then serve immediately with plenty of warm crusty bread.

Budget Tip
Using cheaper cuts of meat in stews and soups like this is a great way of saving money on meat. This flavoursome soup was once a staple Welsh dish, originally made with scraps of mutton or lamb and vegetables cooked together in a broth.

Roasted Aubergine Dip with Pitta Strips

Ingredients (Serves 4)

4 pitta breads
2 large aubergines/eggplants
1 garlic clove, peeled
¼ tsp sesame oil
1 tbsp lemon juice
½ tsp ground cumin
salt and freshly ground black pepper
2 tbsp freshly chopped parsley
fresh salad leaves, to serve

Preheat the oven to 180°C/350°F/Gas Mark 4. On a chopping/cutting board, cut the pitta breads into strips. Spread the bread in a single layer on to a large baking tray.

Cook in the preheated oven for 15 minutes until golden and crisp. Leave to cool on a wire cooling rack.

Trim the aubergines, rinse lightly and reserve. Heat a griddle pan until almost smoking. Cook the aubergines and garlic for about 15 minutes.

Turn the aubergines frequently, until very tender with wrinkled and charred skins. Remove from heat. Leave to cool.

When the aubergines are cool enough to handle, cut in half and scoop out the cooked flesh and place in a food processor.

Squeeze the softened garlic flesh from the papery skin and add to the aubergine.

Blend the aubergine and garlic until smooth, then add the sesame oil, lemon juice and cumin and blend again to mix.

Season to taste with salt and pepper, stir in the parsley and serve with the pitta strips and mixed salad leaves.

Hot Herby Mushrooms

Ingredients (Serves 4)

4 thin slices white bread, crusts removed
125 g/1¼ cups chestnut mushrooms, wiped
    and sliced
125 g/1¼ cups oyster mushrooms, wiped
1 garlic clove, peeled and crushed
1 tsp Dijon mustard
300 ml/½ pt/1¼ cups chicken stock
salt and freshly ground black pepper
1 tbsp freshly chopped parsley
1 tbsp freshly snipped chives, plus
    extra to garnish
mixed salad leaves, to serve

Preheat the oven to 180°C/350°F/Gas Mark 4. With a rolling pin, roll each piece of bread out as thinly as possible.

Press each piece of bread into a 10 cm/4 inch tartlet tin. Push each piece down firmly , then bake in the preheated oven for 20 minutes.

Place the mushrooms in a frying pan with the garlic, mustard and chicken stock and stir-fry over a moderate heat until the mushrooms are tender and the liquid is reduced by half.

Carefully remove the mushrooms from the frying pan with a slotted spoon and transfer to a heat-resistant dish. Cover with kitchen foil and place in the bottom of the oven to keep the mushrooms warm.

Boil the remaining pan juices until reduced to a thick sauce. Season with salt and pepper.

Stir the parsley and the chives into the mushroom mixture.

Place one bread tartlet case on each plate and divide the mushroom mixture between them.

Spoon over the pan juices, garnish with the chives and serve immediately with mixed salad leaves.

Beetroot Ravioli with Dill Cream Sauce

Ingredients (Serves 4-6)

FOR THE PASTA:
225 g/8 oz/1¹⁄₈ cups strong plain bread flour
   or type 00 pasta flour, plus extra for rolling
1 tsp salt
2 medium/large eggs
1 medium/large egg yolk
1 tbsp extra virgin olive oil

FOR THE FILLING:
1 tbsp olive oil
1 small onion, peeled and finely chopped
¹⁄₂ tsp caraway seeds
175 g/6 oz/1 cup cooked beetroot, chopped
175 g/6 oz/³⁄₄ cup ricotta cheese
25 g/1 oz/¹⁄₂ cup fresh white breadcrumbs
1 medium/large egg yolk
2 tbsp grated Parmesan cheese
salt and freshly ground black pepper
4 tbsp walnut oil
4 tbsp freshly chopped dill
1 tbsp green peppercorns, drained and
   roughly chopped
6 tbsp crème fraîche

To make the pasta dough, sift the flour and salt into a large bowl, make a well in the centre and add the eggs and yolk, the oil and 1 teaspoon water. Gradually mix to form a soft but not sticky dough, adding a little more flour or water as necessary. Turn out on to a lightly floured surface and knead for 5 minutes, or until smooth and elastic. Wrap in clingfilm/plastic wrap and leave to rest at room temperature for about 30 minutes.

To make the filling, heat the olive oil in a large frying pan, add the onion and caraway seeds and cook over a medium heat for 5 minutes, or until the onion is softened and lightly golden. Stir in the beetroot and cook for 5 minutes.

Blend the beetroot mixture in a food processor until smooth, then allow to cool. Stir in the ricotta cheese, breadcrumbs, egg yolk and Parmesan cheese. Season the filling to taste with salt and pepper and reserve.

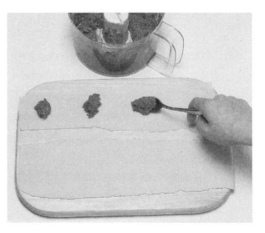

✓ Divide the pasta dough into 8 pieces and either feed each through a pasta machine, or use a rolling pin, to create long thin rectangular sheets. Lay 1 sheet on a floured surface and place 5 heaped teaspoons of the filling 2.5 cm/1 in apart.

✓ Dampen around the heaps of filling and lay a second sheet of pasta over the top. Press around the heaps to seal.

✓ Cut into squares using a pastry wheel or sharp knife. Put the filled pasta shapes on to a floured tea towel.

✓ Bring a large pan of lightly salted water to a rolling boil. Drop the ravioli into the water, return to the boil and cook for 3–4 minutes, until *al dente*.

✓ Meanwhile, heat the walnut oil in a small pan, then add the chopped dill and green peppercorns. Remove from the heat, stir in the crème fraîche and season well. Drain the cooked pasta thoroughly and toss with the sauce. Tip into warmed serving dishes and serve immediately.

Budget Tip
Making your own pasta can save you money. Do not forget that if you make too much dough, you can freeze it – just make sure you take it out of the freezer with enough time for it to thaw (it will take around a day to thaw in the fridge).

Gnocchi with Grilled Cherry Tomatoes

Ingredients (Serves 4)

450 g/1 lb floury potatoes, unpeeled
1 medium/large egg
1 tsp salt
75–90 g/3–3¹/₂ oz/¹/₂ cup plain/all-purpose flour
450 g/1 lb mixed red and orange cherry tomatoes,
    halved lengthways
2 garlic cloves, peeled and finely sliced
zest of ¹/₂ lemon, finely grated
1 tbsp freshly chopped thyme
1 tbsp freshly chopped basil
2 tbsp extra virgin olive oil, plus extra for drizzling
salt and freshly ground black pepper
pinch of sugar
freshly grated Parmesan cheese, to serve

Preheat the grill just before required. Bring a large pan of salted water to the boil, add the potatoes and cook for 20–25 minutes until tender. Drain. Leave until cool enough to handle but still hot, then peel them and place in a large bowl. Mash until smooth, then work in the egg, salt and enough of the flour to form a soft dough.

With floured hands, roll a spoonful of the dough into a small ball. Flatten the ball slightly on to the back of a large fork, then roll it off the fork to make a little ridged dumpling. Place each gnocchi on to a floured tea towel as you work.

Place the tomatoes in a flameproof shallow dish. Add the garlic, lemon zest, herbs and olive oil. Season to taste with salt and pepper and sprinkle over the sugar. Cook under the preheated grill for 10 minutes, or until the tomatoes are charred and tender, stirring once or twice.

Meanwhile, bring a large pan of lightly salted water to the boil, then reduce to a simmer. Dropping in 6–8 gnocchi at a time, cook in batches for 3–4 minutes, or until they begin bobbing up to the surface. Remove with a slotted spoon and drain well on absorbent kitchen paper before transferring to a warmed serving dish; cover with foil. Toss the cooked gnocchi with the tomato sauce. Serve immediately with a little Parmesan.

Budget Tip
Making gnocchi from scratch can save you money. If you make too, many you can freeze them: put them on a baking tray in the freezer and, when frozen, transfer them to a bag or container. Cook straight from frozen.

French Onion Tart

Ingredients (Serves 4)

FOR QUICK FLAKY PASTRY:
125 g/4 oz/¹/₂ cup butter
175 g/6 oz/1¹/₂ cups plain/all-purpose flour
pinch of salt

FOR THE FILLING:
2 tbsp olive oil
4 large onions, peeled and thinly sliced
3 tbsp white wine vinegar
2 tbsp muscovado/dark brown sugar
a little beaten egg or milk
175 g/6 oz/1¹/₂ cups Cheddar cheese, grated
salt and freshly ground black pepper

Preheat the oven to 200°C/400°F/Gas Mark 6. Place the butter in the freezer for 30 minutes. Sift the flour and salt into a large bowl. Grate the butter on the coarse side of a grater, dipping the butter in the flour every now and again as it makes it easier to grate. Mix the butter into the flour, using a knife, making sure all the butter is coated thoroughly with flour.

Add 2 tablespoons cold water and continue to mix, bringing the mixture together. Use your hands to complete the mixing. Add a little more water, if needed, to leave a clean bowl. Place the pastry in a polythene bag and chill in the refrigerator for 30 minutes.

Heat the oil in a large frying pan, then fry the onions for 10 minutes, stirring occasionally until softened. Stir in the white wine vinegar and sugar. Increase the heat and stir frequently for another 4 minutes until the onions turn a deep caramel colour. Cook for another 5 minutes, then reserve to cool.

On a lightly floured surface, roll out the pastry to a 35.5 cm/14 inch circle. Wrap over a rolling pin and move to a baking sheet. Sprinkle half the cheese, and the onions, over the pastry, leaving a 5 cm/2 inch border around the edge. Fold the pastry edges over the edge of the filling to form a rim and brush the rim with beaten egg or milk. Season to taste with salt and pepper. Sprinkle over the remaining Cheddar and bake for 20–25 minutes. Transfer to a large plate and serve immediately.

Recipes:
Fish &
Seafood

PACKED WITH
• MONEY •
SAVING
• IDEAS & TIPS •

Barbecued Fish Kebabs

Ingredients (Serves 4)

8 skewers
450 g/1 lb herring or mackerel fillets, cut
  into chunks
2 small red onions, peeled and quartered
16 cherry tomatoes
salt and freshly ground black pepper
freshly cooked couscous, to serve

FOR THE SAUCE:
150 ml/¼ pt/⅔ cup fish stock
5 tbsp ketchup
2 tbsp Worcestershire sauce
2 tbsp wine vinegar
2 tbsp brown sugar
2 drops Tabasco/hot chilli sauce
2 tbsp tomato puree/paste

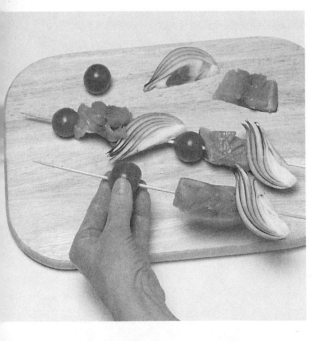

Line a grill/broiler rack with a single layer of kitchen foil and preheat the grill at a high temperature, 2 minutes before use.

If using wooden skewers, soak in cold water for 30 minutes to prevent them from catching alight during cooking.

Meanwhile, prepare the sauce. Add the fish stock, tomato ketchup, Worcestershire sauce, vinegar, sugar, Tabasco and tomato puree to a small saucepan. Stir well and leave to simmer for 5 minutes.

When ready to cook, drain the skewers, if necessary, then thread the fish chunks, the quartered red onions and the cherry tomatoes alternately on to the skewers.

Season the kebabs to taste with salt and pepper and brush with the sauce. Grill under the preheated grill for 8–10 minutes, basting with the sauce occasionally. Turn the kebabs often to ensure that they are cooked thoroughly and evenly on all sides. Serve immediately with couscous.

Spicy Sardines

Ingredients (Serves 4-6)

8–12 fresh sardines, depending on size
2 tbsp lime juice
2.5-cm/1-in piece fresh root ginger, peeled
   and grated
3 garlic cloves, peeled and crushed
1 tsp ground coriander/cilantro
1 tsp ground cumin
1 tbsp Madras/medium-hot curry paste
2–3 tbsp vegetable oil
lime wedges, to garnish

TO SERVE:
dhal (optional, see page 239)
green salad

Lightly rinse the sardines and pat dry with absorbent kitchen paper. Make diagonal slashes across both sides of the sardines and reserve.

Blend the lime juice, ginger, garlic, ground coriander, cumin and curry paste together.

Lightly smear the mixture over the fish. Leave in the refrigerator until required.

Heat the oil in a large nonstick frying pan, add the sardines, in batches depending on size, and cook for 2–4 minutes on each side. Remove, garnish with the lime wedges and serve with dhal and a green salad.

Tasty Tip
If liked, the sardines can be grilled/broiled. Place on a foil-lined rack and cook under a preheated medium-hot grill for 6–8 minutes, or until cooked.

Citrus-grilled Plaice

Ingredients (Serves 4)

1 tsp sunflower oil
1 onion, peeled and chopped
1 orange pepper, deseeded and chopped
175 g/6 oz/³/₄ cup long-grain rice
150 ml/¹/₄ pt/²/₃ cup orange juice
2 tbsp lemon juice
225 ml/8 fl oz/1 cup vegetable stock
spray of oil
4 x 175 g/6 oz plaice/flounder fillets, skinned
1 orange
1 lemon
25 g/1 oz/¹/₄ stick half-fat butter or low-fat spread
2 tbsp freshly chopped tarragon
salt and freshly ground black pepper
lemon wedges, to garnish

Heat the oil in a large frying pan, then sauté the onion, pepper and rice for 2 minutes.

Add the orange and lemon juice and bring to the boil. Reduce the heat, add half the stock and simmer for 15–20 minutes, or until the rice is tender, adding the remaining stock as necessary.

Preheat the grill/broiler. Finely spray the base of the grill pan with oil. Place the fish in the base and reserve.

Finely grate the orange and lemon rind. Squeeze the juice from half of each fruit.

Melt the butter or low-fat spread in a small saucepan. Add the grated rind, juice and half the tarragon and use to baste the plaice fillets.

Cook one side only of the fish under the preheated grill at a medium heat for 4–6 minutes, basting continuously.

Once the rice is cooked, stir in the remaining tarragon and season to taste with salt and pepper. Garnish the fish with the lemon wedges and serve immediately with the rice.

Cheesy Vegetable and Prawn Bake

Ingredients (Serves 4)

175 g/6 oz/1 cup long-grain rice
salt and freshly ground black pepper
1 garlic clove, peeled and crushed
1 large/extra-large egg, beaten
3 tbsp freshly shredded basil
4 tbsp Parmesan cheese, grated
125 g/4 oz baby asparagus spears, trimmed
150 g/5 oz/1 cup baby carrots, trimmed
150 g/5 oz/1 cup fine green beans, trimmed
150 g/5 oz/1 cup cherry tomatoes
175 g/6 oz/1 cup peeled prawns/shrimp,
    thawed if frozen
125 g/4 oz mozzarella cheese, thinly sliced

Preheat the oven to 200°C/400°F/Gas Mark 6, about 10 minutes before required. Cook the rice in lightly salted boiling water for 12–15 minutes, or until tender, then drain. Stir in the garlic, beaten egg, shredded basil and 2 tablespoons of the Parmesan cheese and season to

taste with salt and pepper. Press this mixture into a greased 23-cm/9-in square ovenproof dish and reserve.

Bring a large saucepan of water to the boil, then drop in the asparagus, carrots and green beans. Return to the boil and cook for 3–4 minutes. Drain and leave to cool.

Quarter or halve the cherry tomatoes and mix them Into the cooled vegetables. Spread the prepared vegetables over the rice and top with the prawns. Season to taste with salt and pepper.

Cover the prawns with the mozzarella and sprinkle over the remaining Parmesan cheese. Bake in the preheated oven for 20–25 minutes until piping hot and golden brown in places. Serve immediately.

Budget Tip
Small frozen cooked prawns/shrimp are likely to be less expensive than large fresh prawns, and cow's-milk mozzarella should cost less than authentic buffalo mozzarella.

Traditional Fish Pie

Ingredients (Serves 4)

450 g/1 lb cod or coley fillets, skinned
450 ml/³⁄₄ pt/1¹⁄₄ cups milk
1 small onion, peeled and quartered
salt and freshly ground black pepper
900 g/2 lb/8 cups potatoes, peeled and cut into chunks
100 g/3¹⁄₂ oz/¹⁄₄ cup and 3 tbsp butter
125 g/4 oz/¹⁄₄ lb large prawns/shrimp
2 large/extra-large eggs, hard-boiled and quartered
198 g/7 oz can sweetcorn, drained
2 tbsp freshly chopped parsley
3 tbsp plain/all-purpose flour
50 g/2 oz/¹⁄₂ cup Cheddar cheese, grated

for 8–10 minutes until the fish is cooked. Remove the fish with a slotted spoon and place in a baking dish. Strain the cooking liquid and reserve.

Boil the potatoes until soft, then mash with 3 tablespoons of the butter and 2–3 tablespoons of the remaining milk. Reserve.

Arrange the prawns and eggs on top of the fish, then scatter over the sweetcorn and sprinkle with the parsley.

Preheat the oven to 200°C/400°F/Gas Mark 6, about 15 minutes before cooking. Place the fish in a shallow frying pan, pour over 300 ml/¹⁄₂ pt/1¹⁄₄ cups of the milk and add the onion. Season to taste with salt and pepper. Bring to the boil and simmer

Melt the remaining butter in a saucepan, stir in the flour and cook gently for 1 minute, stirring. Whisk in the reserved cooking liquid and remaining milk. Cook for 2 minutes, or until thickened, then pour over the fish mixture and cool slightly.

Spread the mashed potato over the top of the pie and sprinkle over the grated cheese. Bake in the preheated oven for 30 minutes until golden. Serve immediately.

Tasty Tip

Any variety of white fish may be used in this delicious dish, including haddock, hake, ling, pollack and whiting. You could also used smoked fish, such as smoked cod or haddock for a change. After simmering in milk, carefully check and remove any bones from the cooked fish.

Coconut Fish Curry

Ingredients (Serves 4)

2 tbsp sunflower oil
1 medium onion, peeled and very finely chopped
1 yellow pepper, deseeded and finely chopped
1 garlic clove, peeled and crushed
1 tbsp mild curry paste
2.5-cm/1-in piece root ginger, peeled and grated
1 red chilli, deseeded and finely chopped
400 ml/14 oz can coconut milk
700 g/1½ lb firm white fish, e.g. monkfish fillets,
    skinned and cut into chunks
225 g/8 oz/1⅓ cups basmati rice
1 tbsp freshly chopped coriander/cilantro
1 tbsp mango chutney
salt and freshly ground black pepper

TO GARNISH:
lime wedges
fresh coriander/cilantro sprigs

TO SERVE:
Greek/plain yoghurt
warm naan bread

Put 1 tablespoon of the oil into a large frying pan and cook the onion, pepper and garlic for 5 minutes, or until soft. Add the remaining oil, curry paste, ginger and chilli and cook for a further minute.

Pour in the coconut milk and bring to the boil, reduce the heat and simmer gently for 5 minutes, stirring occasionally. Add the monkfish to the pan and continue to simmer gently for 5–10 minutes, or until the fish is tender, but not overcooked.

Meanwhile, cook the rice in a saucepan of boiling salted water for 15 minutes, or until tender. Drain the rice thoroughly and turn out into a serving dish.

Stir the chopped coriander and chutney gently into the fish curry and season to taste with salt and pepper. Spoon the fish curry over the cooked rice, garnish with lime wedges and coriander sprigs and serve immediately with spoonfuls of Greek yoghurt and warm naan bread.

Marinated Mackerel with Tomato and Basil Salad

Ingredients (Serves 3)

3 mackerel, filleted
3 beefsteak/large tomatoes, sliced
50 g/2 oz/2½ cups watercress
2 oranges, peeled and segmented
75 g/3 oz/¾ cup mozzarella cheese, sliced
2 tbsp basil leaves, shredded
sprig of fresh basil, to garnish

FOR THE MARINADE:
juice of 2 lemons
4 tbsp olive oil
4 tbsp basil leaves

FOR THE DRESSING:
1 tbsp lemon juice
1 tsp Dijon mustard
1 tsp caster/superfine sugar
salt and freshly ground black pepper
5 tbsp olive oil

Remove as many of the fine pin bones as possible from the mackerel fillets, lightly rinse and pat dry with absorbent kitchen paper and place in a shallow dish.

Blend the marinade ingredients together and pour over the mackerel fillets. Make sure the marinade has covered the fish completely. Cover and leave in a cool place for at least 8 hours, but preferably overnight.

As the fillets marinate, they will lose the translucency and look as if they are cooked.

Place the tomatoes, watercress, oranges and mozzarella cheese in a large bowl and toss.

To make the dressing, whisk the lemon juice with the mustard, sugar and seasoning in a bowl. Pour over half the dressing, toss again and then arrange on a serving platter. Remove the mackerel from the marinade, cut into bite-sized pieces and sprinkle with the shredded basil. Arrange on top of the salad, drizzle over the remaining dressing, scatter with basil leaves and garnish with a basil sprig. Serve.

Tagliatelle with Tuna and Anchovy Tapenade

Ingredients (Serves 4)

400 g/14 oz tagliatelle
125 g/4 oz can tuna fish in oil, drained
50 g/2 oz can anchovy fillets, drained
150 g/5 oz/1¼ cups pitted black olives
2 tbsp capers in brine, drained
2 tsp lemon juice
100 ml/3½ fl oz/⅓ cup olive oil
2 tbsp freshly chopped parsley
freshly ground black pepper
sprigs of flat-leaf parsley, to garnish

☑ Bring a large pan of lightly salted water to a rolling boil. Add the tagliatelle and cook according to the packet instructions, or until *al dente*.

☑ Meanwhile, place the tuna fish, anchovy fillets, olives and capers in a food processor with the lemon juice and 2 tablespoons of the olive oil and blend for a few seconds until roughly chopped.

☑ With the motor running, pour in the remaining olive oil in a steady stream; the resulting mixture should be slightly chunky rather than smooth.

☑ Spoon the sauce into a bowl, stir in the chopped parsley and season to taste with black pepper. Check the taste of the sauce and add a little more lemon juice, if required.

☑ Drain the pasta thoroughly. Pour the sauce into the pan and cook over a low heat for 1–2 minutes to warm through.

☑ Return the drained pasta to the pan and mix together with the sauce. Tip into a warmed serving bowl or spoon on to warm individual plates. Garnish with sprigs of flat-leaf parsley and serve immediately.

Smoked Mackerel and Pasta Frittata

Ingredients (Serves 4)

25 g/1 oz/¼ cup tricolore pasta spirals or shells
225 g/8 oz smoked mackerel (or salmon)
6 medium/large eggs
3 tbsp milk
2 tsp wholegrain mustard
2 tbsp freshly chopped parsley
salt and freshly ground black pepper
25 g/1 oz/¼ stick unsalted butter
6 spring onions/scallions, trimmed and
    diagonally sliced
50 g/2 oz/½ cup frozen peas, thawed
75 g/3 oz/¾ cup mature Cheddar cheese, grated

TO SERVE:
green salad
warm crusty bread

Preheat the grill/broiler to high just before cooking. Bring a pan of lightly salted water to a rolling boil. Add the pasta and cook according to the packet instructions, or until *al dente*. Drain thoroughly and reserve.

Remove the skin from the mackerel and break the fish into large flakes, discarding any bones, and reserve.

Place the eggs, milk, mustard and parsley in a bowl and whisk together. Season with just a little salt and plenty of freshly ground black pepper and reserve.

Melt the butter in a large, heavy-based frying pan. Cook the spring onions gently for 3–4 minutes, until soft. Pour in the egg mixture, then add the drained pasta, peas and half the mackerel. Gently stir the mixture in the pan for 1–2 minutes, or until beginning to set. Stop stirring and cook for about 1 minute until the underneath is golden brown.

Scatter the remaining mackerel over the frittata, followed by the grated cheese. Place under the preheated grill for about 1½ minutes, or until golden brown and set. Cut into wedges and serve immediately with salad and crusty bread.

Ratatouille Mackerel

Ingredients (Serves 4)

1 red pepper/bell pepper
1 tbsp olive oil
1 red onion, peeled
1 garlic clove, peeled and thinly sliced
2 courgettes/zucchini, trimmed and
    cut into thick slices
400 g/14 oz can chopped tomatoes
sea salt and freshly ground black pepper
4 x 275 g/10 oz small mackerel, cleaned
    and heads removed
spray of olive oil
lemon juice for drizzling
12 fresh basil leaves
couscous or rice mixed with chopped
    parsley, to serve

Preheat the oven to 190°C/375°F/Gas Mark 5. Cut the top off the red pepper, remove the seeds and membrane, then cut into chunks. Cut the red onion into thick wedges.

Heat the oil in a large pan and cook the onion and garlic for 5 minutes or until beginning to soften. Add the pepper chunks and courgette slices and cook for a further 5 minutes.

Pour in the chopped tomatoes with juice and cook for a further 5 minutes. Season to taste with salt and pepper and pour into an ovenproof dish.

Season the fish with salt and pepper and arrange on top of the vegetables. Spray with a little olive oil and lemon juice. Cover and cook in the preheated oven for 20 minutes.

Remove the cover, add the basil leaves and return to the oven for a further 5 minutes. Serve immediately with couscous or rice mixed with parsley.

Food Fact

Ratatouille is a traditional French dish using onions, tomatoes, courgettes/zucchini and often aubergine/eggplant. It is a very versatile dish to which many other vegetables can be added. For that extra kick, why not add a little chopped chilli?

Fettuccine with Sardines and Spinach

Ingredients (Serves 4)

125 g/4 oz can sardines in olive oil
400 g/14 oz fettuccine or tagliarini
40 g/1½ oz/⅓ cup butter
2 tbsp olive oil
50 g/2 oz/1 cup one-day-old white breadcrumbs
1 garlic clove, peeled and finely chopped
50 g/2 oz/½ cup pine nuts
125 g/4 oz/1 cup chestnut mushrooms, wiped and sliced
125 g/4 oz/1½ cups baby spinach leaves, rinsed
150 ml/¼ pt/⅔ cup crème fraîche
rind of 1 lemon, finely grated
salt and freshly ground black pepper

Drain the sardines and cut in half lengthways. Remove the bones, then cut the fish into 2.5-cm/1-in pieces and reserve.

Bring a large pan of lightly salted water to a rolling boil. Add the pasta and cook according to the packet instructions, or until *al dente*.

Meanwhile, melt half the butter with the olive oil in a large saucepan, add the breadcrumbs and fry, stirring, until they begin to turn crisp. Add the garlic and pine nuts and continue to cook until golden brown. Remove from the pan and reserve. Wipe the pan clean.

Melt the remaining butter in the pan, add the mushrooms and cook for 4–5 minutes, or until soft. Add the spinach and cook, stirring, for 1 minute, or until beginning to wilt. Stir in the crème fraîche and lemon rind and bring to the boil. Simmer gently until the spinach is just cooked. Season the sauce to taste with salt and pepper.

Drain the pasta thoroughly and return to the pan. Add the spinach sauce and sardine pieces and gently toss together. Tip into a warmed serving dish. Sprinkle with the toasted breadcrumbs and pine nuts and serve immediately.

Sweet-and-sour Fish

Ingredients (Serves 4)

1 small carrot, peeled and cut into julienne strips
1 small red or green pepper/bell pepper
125 g/4 oz/³/₄ cup mangetout/snow peas, cut in
 half diagonally
125 g/4 oz/1 cup frozen peas, thawed
2–3 spring onions/scallions, trimmed and sliced
 diagonally into 5-cm/2-in pieces
450 g/1 lb small thin skinless plaice/flounder fillets
1¹/₂–2 tbsp cornflour/cornstarch
vegetable oil for frying
sprigs of fresh coriander/cilantro, to garnish

FOR THE SWEET-AND-SOUR SAUCE:
2 tsp cornflour/cornstarch
300 ml/¹/₂ pt/1¹/₄ cups fish or chicken stock
4-cm/1¹/₂-in piece fresh root ginger, peeled and
 finely sliced
2 tbsp soy sauce
2 tbsp rice wine vinegar or dry sherry
2 tbsp ketchup or tomato concentrate
2 tbsp Chinese rice vinegar or cider vinegar
1¹/₂ tbsp soft light brown sugar

Make the sauce. Place the cornflour in a saucepan and gradually whisk in the stock. Stir in the remaining sauce ingredients and bring to the boil, stirring, until the sauce thickens. Simmer for 2 minutes, then remove from the heat and reserve.

Bring a saucepan of water to the boil. Add the carrot, return to the boil and cook for 3 minutes. Add the pepper and cook for 1 minute. Add the mangetout and peas and cook for 30 seconds. Drain, rinse under cold water and drain again. Add to the sweet-and-sour sauce with the spring onions.

Using a sharp knife, make crisscross slashes across the top of each fish fillet, then lightly coat on both sides with the cornflour. Pour enough oil into a large wok to come 5 cm/2 in up the side. Heat to 190°C/375°F, or until a cube of bread browns in 30 seconds. Fry the fillets, 2 at a time, for 3–5 minutes, until crisp and golden, turning once. Remove and drain on absorbent kitchen paper. Bring the sweet-and-sour sauce to the boil, stirring constantly. Serve the fish with the sauce and garnish.

Spaghetti alla Puttanesca

Ingredients (Serves 4)

4 tbsp olive oil
50 g/2 oz can anchovy fillets in olive oil,
  drained and coarsely chopped
2 garlic cloves, peeled and finely chopped
1/2 tsp crushed dried chillies
400 g/14 oz can chopped plum tomatoes
125 g/4 oz pitted black olives, cut in half
2 tbsp capers, rinsed and drained
1 tsp freshly chopped oregano
1 tbsp tomato paste
salt and freshly ground black pepper
400 g/14 oz spaghetti
2 tbsp freshly chopped parsley

Heat the olive oil in a large frying pan, add the anchovies and cook, stirring with a wooden spoon and crushing the anchovies, until they disintegrate. Add the garlic and dried chillies and cook for 1 minute, stirring frequently.

Add the tomatoes, olives, capers, oregano and tomato paste and cook, stirring occasionally, for 15 minutes, or until the liquid has evaporated and the sauce has thickened. Season the tomato sauce to taste with salt and pepper.

Meanwhile, bring a large pan of lightly salted water to a rolling boil. Add the spaghetti and cook according to the packet instructions, or until *al dente*.

Drain the spaghetti thoroughly, reserving 1–2 tablespoons of the cooking water. Return the spaghetti with the reserved water to the pan. Pour the tomato sauce over the spaghetti, add the chopped parsley and toss to coat. Tip into a warmed serving dish or spoon on to individual plates and serve immediately.

Budget Tip

This is a great back-up recipe – everything in it, except the fresh herbs (which you could live without), should be in your store cupboard, for those days when your fridge is on the empty side.

Recipes: Meat & Poultry

PACKED WITH
MONEY
SAVING
IDEAS & TIPS

Pork Cabbage Parcels

Ingredients (Serves 4)

8 large green cabbage leaves
1 tbsp vegetable oil
2 celery stalks, trimmed and chopped
1 carrot, peeled and cut into matchsticks
125 g/4 oz fresh minced/ground pork
50 g/2 oz/½ cup button mushrooms, wiped
  and sliced
1 tsp Chinese five-spice powder
50 g/2 oz/¼ cup cooked long-grain rice
juice of 1 lemon
1 tbsp soy sauce
150 ml/¼ pt/⅔ cup chicken stock

FOR THE TOMATO SAUCE:
1 tbsp vegetable oil
1 bunch spring onions/scallions, trimmed
  and chopped
400 g/14 oz can chopped tomatoes
1 tbsp light soy sauce
1 tbsp freshly chopped mint
freshly ground black pepper

Preheat the oven to 180°C/350°F/Gas Mark 4, 10 minutes before cooking. To make the sauce, heat the oil in a heavy-based saucepan, add the spring onions and cook for 2 minutes, or until softened. Add the tomatoes, soy sauce and mint to the saucepan, bring to the boil, cover, then simmer for 10 minutes. Season to taste with pepper. Reheat when required.

Meanwhile, blanch the cabbage leaves in a large saucepan of lightly salted water for 3 minutes. Drain and refresh under cold running water. Pat dry with absorbent kitchen paper and reserve.

Heat the oil in a small saucepan, add the celery, carrot and pork and cook for 3 minutes. Add the mushrooms and cook for 3 minutes. Stir in the Chinese five-spice powder, rice, lemon juice and soy sauce and heat through.

Place some of the filling in the centre of each cabbage leaf and fold to enclose the filling. Place in a shallow ovenproof dish seam-side down. Pour over the stock and cook in the preheated oven for 30 minutes. Serve immediately with the reheated tomato sauce.

Sausage and Bacon Risotto

Ingredients (Serves 4)

225 g/8 oz/1⅛ cup long-grain rice
1 tbsp olive oil
25 g/1 oz/¼ stick butter
4 cocktail or small link sausages
1 shallot, peeled and finely chopped
75 g/3 oz/⅓ cup bacon lardons or thick slices
    of streaky bacon, chopped
150 g/5 oz/1¼ cups chorizo or similar spicy
    sausage, cut into chunks
1 green pepper/bell pepper, deseeded and cut
    into strips
197 g/7 oz can sweetcorn, drained
2 tbsp freshly chopped parsley
50 g/2 oz/⅓ cup mozzarella cheese, grated

Cook the rice in a saucepan of boiling salted water for 15 minutes or until tender, or according to packet instructions. Drain and rinse in cold water. Drain again and leave until completely cold.

Meanwhile, heat the wok, pour in the oil and melt the butter. Cook the cocktail sausages, turning continuously until cooked. Remove with a slotted spoon, cut in half and keep warm.

Add the chopped shallot and bacon to the wok and cook for 2–3 minutes until cooked but not browned. Add the spicy sausage and green pepper and stir-fry for a further 3 minutes.

Add the cold rice and the sweetcorn to the wok and stir-fry for 2 minutes, then return the cooked sausages to the wok and stir over the heat until everything is piping hot. Garnish with the freshly chopped parsley and serve immediately with a little grated mozzarella cheese.

Helpful Hint

It is now possible to buy packets of bacon or pancetta lardons but, if these are unavailable, try to get bacon in a piece from a butcher or deli. Cut the bacon into 1-cm/½-in slices, then cut the slices crossways into 1-cm/½-in pieces.

Spaghetti Bolognese

Ingredients (Serves 4)

1 carrot
2 celery stalks
1 onion
2 garlic cloves
450 g/1 lb lean minced/ground beef steak
225 g/8 oz/2 cups smoked streaky bacon, chopped
1 tbsp plain/all-purpose flour
150 ml/5 fl oz/²/₃ cup red wine
400 g/14 oz can chopped tomatoes
2 tbsp tomato puree/paste
2 tsp dried mixed herbs
salt and freshly ground black pepper
pinch of sugar
350 g/12 oz/4 cups spaghetti
sprigs of fresh oregano, to garnish
shavings of Parmesan cheese, to serve

Peel and chop the carrot, trim and chop the celery, then peel and chop

the onion and garlic. Heat a large non-stick frying pan and sauté the beef and bacon for 5–10 minutes, stirring occasionally, until browned. Add the prepared vegetables to the frying pan and cook for about 3 minutes, or until softened, stirring occasionally.

Add the flour and cook for 1 minute. Stir in the red wine, tomatoes, tomato puree, mixed herbs, seasoning to taste and sugar. Bring to the boil, then cover and simmer for 45 minutes, stirring occasionally.

Meanwhile, bring a large saucepan of lightly salted water to the boil and cook the spaghetti for 10–12 minutes, or until *al dente*. Drain well and divide between four serving plates. Spoon over the sauce, garnish with a few sprigs of oregano and serve immediately with plenty of Parmesan shavings.

Budget Tip
If you prefer, replace the wine with beef stock and add a little Worcestershire sauce for more flavour.

Meatballs with Olives

Ingredients (Serves 4)

250 g/9 oz/1 cup shallots, peeled
2–3 garlic cloves, peeled
450 g/1 lb minced/ground beef
2 tbsp fresh white or wholemeal breadcrumbs
3 tbsp freshly chopped basil
salt and freshly ground black pepper
2 tbsp olive oil
5 tbsp ready-made pesto sauce
5 tbsp mascarpone or cream cheese
5 tbsp pitted black olives, halved
275 g/10 oz/3¾ cups thick pasta noodles
freshly chopped flat-leaf parsley
sprigs of fresh flat-leaf parsley, to garnish
freshly grated Parmesan cheese, to serve

Chop 2 of the shallots finely and place in a bowl with the garlic, beef, breadcrumbs, basil and seasoning to taste. With damp hands, bring the mixture together and shape into small balls about the size of an apricot.

Heat the olive oil in a frying pan and cook the meatballs for 8–10 minutes, turning occasionally, until browned and the beef is tender. Remove and drain on absorbent kitchen paper.

Slice the remaining shallots, add to the pan and cook for 5 minutes, until softened. Blend the pesto and mascarpone or cream cheese together, then stir into the pan with the olives. Bring to the boil, reduce the heat and return the meatballs to the pan. Simmer for 5–8 minutes, or until the sauce has thickened and the meatballs are cooked thoroughly.

Meanwhile, bring a large saucepan of lightly salted water to the boil and cook the noodles for 8–10 minutes, or until al dente. Drain the noodles, reserving 2 tablespoons of the cooking liquor. Return the noodles to the pan with the reserved cooking liquor and pour in the sauce. Stir the noodles, then sprinkle with chopped parsley. Garnish with a few sprigs of parsley and serve immediately with grated Parmesan cheese.

Traditional Lasagne

Ingredients (Serves 4)

450 g/1 lb lean minced/ground beef
175 g/6 oz/³/₄ cup pancetta or smoked streaky
  bacon, chopped
1 large onion, peeled and chopped
2 celery stalks, trimmed and chopped
125 g/4 oz/1 cup button mushrooms, wiped
  and chopped
2 garlic cloves, peeled and chopped
90 g/3¹/₂ oz/1 cup plain/all-purpose flour
300 ml/¹/₂ pt/1¹/₄ cups beef stock
1 tbsp freeze-dried mixed herbs
5 tbsp tomato puree/paste
salt and freshly ground black pepper
75 g/3 oz/¹/₂ stick butter
1 tsp English mustard powder
pinch of freshly grated nutmeg
900 ml/1¹/₂ pts/scant qt milk
125 g/4 oz/1¹/₄ cups Parmesan cheese, grated
125 g/4 oz/1 cup Cheddar cheese, grated
8–12 precooked lasagne sheets

TO SERVE:
crusty bread
fresh green salad leaves

Preheat oven to 200°C/400°F/Gas Mark 6, 15 minutes before cooking. Cook the beef and pancetta in a large saucepan for 10 minutes, stirring to break up any lumps. Add the onion, celery and mushrooms and cook for 4 minutes, or until slightly softened.

Stir in the garlic and 1 tablespoon of the flour, then cook for 1 minute. Stir in the stock, herbs and tomato puree. Season to taste with salt and pepper.

Bring to the boil, then cover, reduce the heat and simmer for 45 minutes.

Meanwhile, melt the butter in a small saucepan and stir in the remaining flour, mustard powder and nutmeg, until well blended. Cook for 2 minutes. Remove from the heat and gradually blend in the milk until smooth. Return to the heat and bring to the boil, stirring, until thickened. Gradually stir in half the Parmesan and Cheddar cheeses until melted. Season to taste.

Spoon half the meat mixture into the base of a large ovenproof dish. Top with a single layer of pasta. Spread over half the sauce and scatter with half the cheese. Repeat layers, finishing with cheese. Bake in the preheated oven for 30 minutes, or until the pasta is cooked and the top is golden brown and bubbly. Serve immediately with crusty bread and a green salad.

Chilli Con Carne with Crispy-skinned Potatoes

Ingredients (Serves 4)

2 tbsp vegetable oil, plus extra for brushing
1 large onion, peeled and finely chopped
1 garlic clove, peeled and finely chopped
1 red chilli, deseeded and finely chopped
450 g/1 lb chuck steak, finely chopped, or lean minced/ground beef
1 tbsp chilli powder
400 g/14 oz can chopped tomatoes
2 tbsp tomato puree/paste
400 g/14 oz can red kidney beans, drained and rinsed
4 large baking potatoes
coarse salt and freshly ground black pepper

TO SERVE:
ready-made guacamole
sour cream

Preheat the oven to 150°C/300°F/Gas Mark 2. Heat the oil in a large flameproof casserole and add the onion. Cook gently for 10 minutes until soft and lightly browned. Add the garlic and chilli and cook briefly. Increase the heat. Add the beef and cook for a further 10 minutes, stirring occasionally, until browned.

Add the chilli powder and stir well. Cook for about 2 minutes, then add the chopped tomatoes and tomato puree. Bring slowly to the boil. Cover and cook in the preheated oven for

1½ hours. Remove from the oven and stir in the kidney beans. Return to the oven for a further 15 minutes.

Meanwhile, brush a little vegetable oil all over the potatoes and rub on some coarse salt. Put the potatoes in the oven alongside the chilli.

Remove the chilli and potatoes from the oven. Cut a cross in each potato, then squeeze to open slightly and season to taste with salt and pepper. Serve with the chilli, guacamole and sour cream.

Shepherd's Pie

Ingredients (Serves 4)

2 tbsp vegetable or olive oil
1 onion, peeled and finely chopped
1 carrot, peeled and finely chopped
1 celery stalk, trimmed and finely chopped
1 tbsp sprigs of fresh thyme
450 g/1 lb leftover roast lamb, finely chopped
150 ml/¼ pt/⅔ cup red wine
150 ml/¼ pt/⅔ cup lamb or vegetable stock
2 tbsp tomato puree/paste
salt and freshly ground black pepper
700 g/1½ lb potatoes, peeled and cut into chunks
25 g/¼ stick butter
6 tbsp milk
1 tbsp freshly chopped parsley
fresh herbs, to garnish

Preheat the oven to 200°C/400°F/Gas Mark 6, about 15 minutes before cooking. Heat the oil in a large saucepan and add the onion, carrot and celery. Cook over a medium heat for 8–10 minutes until softened and starting to brown. Add the thyme and cook briefly, then add the cooked lamb, wine, stock and tomato puree. Season to taste with salt and pepper and simmer gently for 25–30 minutes until reduced and thickened. Remove from the heat to cool slightly and season again.

Meanwhile, boil the potatoes in plenty of salted water for 12–15 minutes until tender. Drain and return to the saucepan over a low heat to dry out. Remove from the heat and add the butter, milk and parsley. Mash until creamy, adding a little more milk, if necessary. Adjust the seasoning.

Transfer the lamb mixture to a shallow ovenproof dish. Spoon the mashed potatoes over the filling and spread evenly to cover completely. Fork the surface, place on a baking sheet, then cook in the preheated oven for 25–30 minutes until the potato topping is browned and the filling is piping hot. Garnish and serve.

Budget Tip
Make this with minced/ground lamb if preferred. Simply dry-fry 450 g/1 lb lean minced/ground lamb in a nonstick frying pan over a high heat until well browned, then follow the recipe as before.

Lamb's Liver with Bacon and Onions

Ingredients (Serves 4)

350 g/³/₄ lb lamb's liver
2 heaped tbsp plain/all-purpose flour
salt and freshly ground black pepper
2 tbsp groundnut oil
2 large onions, peeled and finely sliced
2 garlic cloves, peeled and chopped
1 red chilli, deseeded and chopped
175 g/6 oz streaky bacon
40 g/1¹/₂ oz/¹/₃ stick butter
300 ml/¹/₂ pt/1¹/₄ cups lamb or beef stock
2 tbsp freshly chopped parsley

TO SERVE:
freshly cooked mashed potatoes
freshly cooked vegetables

Trim the liver, discarding any sinew or tubes, and slice thinly. Season the flour with salt and pepper, then use to coat the liver; reserve.

Heat a wok, then add the oil and when hot, add the sliced onion, garlic and chilli and cook for 5–6 minutes, or until soft and browned. Remove from the wok with a slotted spoon and reserve. Cut each slice of the bacon in half and stir-fry for 3–4 minutes or until cooked. Remove with a slotted spoon and add to the onions.

Melt the butter in the wok and fry the liver on all sides until browned and crisp. Pour in the stock and allow to bubble fiercely for 1–2 minutes. Return the onions and bacon to the wok, stir thoroughly, then cover. Simmer gently for 10 minutes, or until the liver is tender. Sprinkle with parsley and serve immediately with mashed potatoes and freshly cooked vegetables.

Tasty Tip

For creamy mashed potatoes, peel and cube 450 g/1 lb floury potatoes. Cover with cold water and add salt. Bring to the boil and simmer for 15–20 minutes until tender. Drain well and return to the heat for a few seconds to dry out. Add 3 tablespoons butter and 4 tablespoons full cream milk and season. Mash thoroughly, adding a little more milk, if necessary, until smooth and creamy.

Chinese-style Fried Rice

Ingredients (Serves 4-6)

2–3 tbsp groundnut/peanut oil or vegetable oil
2 small onions, peeled and cut into wedges
2 garlic cloves, peeled and thinly sliced
2.5-cm/1-in piece fresh root ginger, peeled and cut
   into thin slivers
225 g/8 oz/2½ cups cooked chicken, thinly sliced
125 g/4 oz/1¼ cups cooked ham, thinly sliced
350 g/12 oz/1⅓ cups cooked cold long-grain
   white rice
125 g/4 oz/½ cup canned water chestnuts, sliced
225 g/8 oz/1½ cups cooked peeled prawns/
   shrimp (optional)
3 large/extra-large eggs
3 tsp sesame oil
salt and freshly ground black pepper
6 spring onions/scallions, trimmed and sliced into
   1-cm/½-in pieces
2 tbsp dark soy sauce
1 tbsp sweet chilli sauce
2 tbsp freshly chopped coriander/cilantro

TO GARNISH:
2 tbsp chopped roasted peanuts
sprig of fresh coriander/cilantro

Heat a wok or large deep frying pan until very hot, add the oil and heat for 30 seconds. Add the onions and stir-fry for 2 minutes. Stir in the garlic and ginger and cook for 1 minute. Add the cooked sliced chicken and ham and stir-fry for a further 2–3 minutes.

Add the rice, water chestnuts and prawns, if using, with 2 tablespoons of water, and stir-fry for 2 minutes until the rice is heated through.

Beat the eggs with 1 teaspoon of the sesame oil and season to taste with salt and pepper. Make a well in the centre of the rice, then pour in the egg mixture and stir immediately, gradually drawing the rice mixture into the egg, until the egg is cooked.

Add the spring onions, sauces, coriander and a little water, if necessary. Adjust the seasoning and drizzle with the remaining sesame oil. Garnish with the nuts and coriander and serve.

Budget Tip
This recipe is great for using up leftovers – why not experiment and vary the ingredients according to what suits you?

Aromatic Chicken Curry

Ingredients (Serves 4)

125 g/4 oz/²/₃ cup red lentils
2 tsp ground coriander
¹/₂ tsp cumin seeds
2 tsp mild curry paste
1 bay leaf
small strip lemon rind
600 ml/1 pt/2¹/₂ cups chicken or vegetable stock
8 chicken thighs, skinned
175 g/6 oz/³/₄ cup spinach leaves, rinsed
   and shredded
1 tbsp freshly chopped coriander/cilantro
2 tsp lemon juice
salt and freshly ground black pepper

TO SERVE:
freshly cooked rice
low-fat natural/plain yoghurt

Put the lentils in a sieve and rinse thoroughly under cold running water.

Dry-fry the ground coriander and cumin seeds in a large saucepan over a low heat for about 30 seconds. Stir in the curry paste.

Add the lentils to the saucepan with the bay leaf and lemon rind, then pour in the stock.

Stir, then slowly bring to the boil. Turn down the heat, half-cover the pan with a lid and simmer gently for 5 minutes, stirring occasionally.

Secure the chicken thighs with cocktail sticks to keep their shape. Place in the pan and half-cover. Simmer for 15 minutes.

Stir in the shredded spinach and cook for a further 25 minutes or until the chicken is very tender and the sauce is thick.

Remove the bay leaf and lemon rind. Stir in the coriander and lemon juice, then season to taste with salt and pepper. Serve immediately with the rice and a little natural yoghurt.

Chicken Livers and Tomato Sauce with Tagliolini

Ingredients (Serves 4)

50 ml/2 fl oz/¹/₄ cup extra virgin olive oil
1 onion, peeled and finely chopped
2 garlic cloves, peeled and finely chopped
125 ml/4 fl oz/¹/₂ cup dry red wine
2 x 400 g/14 oz cans peeled plum tomatoes with juice
1 tbsp tomato puree/paste
1 tbsp freshly chopped sage or thyme leaves
salt and freshly ground black pepper
350 g/12 oz/4 cups fresh or dried tagliolini, papardelle
    or tagliatelle
25 g/1 oz/¹/₄ stick butter
225 g/8 oz/2 cups fresh chicken livers, trimmed and
    cut in half
plain/all-purpose flour for dusting
sprigs of fresh sage, to garnish (optional)

Heat half the olive oil in a large, deep, heavy-based frying pan and add the onion. Cook, stirring frequently, for 4–5 minutes, or until soft and translucent. Stir in the garlic and cook for a further minute.

Add the red wine and cook, stirring, until the wine is reduced by half, then add the tomatoes, tomato puree and half the sage or thyme. Bring to the boil, stirring to break up the tomatoes. Simmer for 30 minutes, stirring occasionally, or until the sauce has reduced and thickened. Season to taste with salt and pepper.

Bring a large pan of lightly salted water to the boil. Add the pasta and cook for 7–10 minutes, or until *al dente*.

Meanwhile, in a large, heavy-based frying pan, melt the remaining oil and the butter and heat until very hot. Pat the chicken livers dry and dust lightly with a little flour. Add to the pan, a few at a time, and cook for 5 minutes, or until crisp and browned, turning carefully – the livers should still be pink inside.

Drain the pasta well and turn into a large, warmed serving bowl. Stir the livers carefully into the sauce, then pour over the pasta and toss gently to coat. Garnish with a sprig of fresh sage and serve immediately.

Spicy Mexican Chicken

Ingredients (Serves 4)

2 tbsp olive oil
450 g/1 lb minced/ground chicken
1 red onion, peeled and chopped
2 garlic cloves, peeled and chopped
1 red pepper/bell pepper, deseeded and chopped
1–2 tsp hot chilli powder
2 tbsp tomato paste
250 ml/8 fl oz/1 cup chicken stock
salt and freshly ground black pepper
420 g/15 oz can red kidney beans, drained
420 g/15 oz can chilli beans, drained
350 g/12 oz spaghetti

TO SERVE:
Monterey Jack or Cheddar cheese, grated
guacamole
hot chilli salsa

Heat the oil in a large frying pan, add the chicken and cook for 5 minutes, stirring frequently with a wooden spoon to break up any lumps. Add the onion, garlic and pepper and cook for 3 minutes, stirring occasionally. Stir in the chilli powder and cook for a further 2 minutes.

Stir in the tomato paste, pour in the chicken stock and season to taste with salt and pepper. Bring to the boil, reduce the heat and simmer, covered, for 20 minutes.

Add the kidney and chilli beans and cook, stirring occasionally, for 10 minutes, or until the chicken is tender.

Meanwhile, bring a large pan of lightly salted water to a rolling boil. Add the spaghetti and cook according to the packet instructions, or until *al dente*.

Drain the spaghetti thoroughly, arrange on warmed plates and spoon over the chicken and bean mixture. Serve with the grated cheese, guacamole and salsa.

Green Turkey Curry

Ingredients (Serves 4)

4 baby aubergines/eggplants, trimmed and quartered
1 tsp salt
2 tbsp sunflower oil
4 shallots, peeled and halved or quartered if large
2 garlic cloves, peeled and sliced
2 tbsp Thai green curry paste
150 ml/¼ pt/⅔ cup chicken stock
1 tbsp Thai fish sauce
1 tbsp lemon juice
350 g/12 oz/1½ cups boneless, skinless turkey
   breast, cubed
1 red pepper/bell pepper, deseeded and sliced
125 g/4 oz/⅞ cup French/green beans, trimmed
   and halved
25 g/1 oz/⅛ cup creamed coconut
freshly boiled rice or steamed Thai fragrant rice,
   to serve

Place the aubergines into a colander and sprinkle with the salt. Set over a plate or in the sink to drain and leave for 30 minutes. Rinse under cold running water and pat dry on absorbent kitchen paper.

Heat a wok or large frying pan, add the sunflower oil and, when hot, add the shallots and garlic and stir-fry for 3 minutes, or until beginning to brown. Add the curry paste and stir-fry for 1–2 minutes. Pour in the stock, fish sauce and lemon juice and simmer for 10 minutes.

Add the turkey, red pepper and French beans to the wok with the aubergines. Return to the boil, then simmer for 10–15 minutes, or until the turkey and vegetables are tender. Add the creamed coconut and stir until melted and the sauce has thickened. Turn into a warmed serving dish and serve immediately with rice.

Food Fact

Several types of aubergine/eggplant are grown in Thailand. Generally, the Thais prefer the small thin varieties, which have a more delicate flavour. You may find these in Asian shops labelled as Chinese aubergines but, if you are unable to find them, you can also use baby aubergines as suggested here.

Thai Stir-fried Spicy Turkey

Ingredients (Serves 4)

2 tbsp Thai fragrant rice
2 tbsp lemon juice
3–5 tbsp chicken stock
2 tbsp Thai fish sauce
1/2–1 tsp cayenne pepper, or to taste
125 g/4 oz fresh minced/ground turkey
2 shallots, peeled and chopped
1/2 lemon grass stalk, outer leaves discarded, and
   finely sliced
1 lime leaf, finely sliced
1 spring onion/scallion, trimmed and finely chopped
freshly chopped coriander/cilantro, to garnish
12 Chinese leaves, to serve

Place the rice in a small frying pan and cook, stirring constantly, over a medium-high heat for 4–5 minutes, or until the rice is browned. Transfer to a spice grinder or blender and pulse briefly until roughly ground. Reserve.

Place the lemon juice, 3 tablespoons of the stock, the fish sauce and cayenne pepper into a small saucepan and bring to the boil. Add the turkey and return to the boil. Continue cooking over a high heat until the turkey is sealed all over.

Add the shallots to the saucepan with the lemon grass, lime leaf, spring onion and reserved rice. Continue cooking for another 1–2 minutes, or until the turkey is cooked through, adding a little more stock, if necessary, to keep the mixture moist.

Spoon a little of the mixture into each Chinese leaf and arrange on a serving dish or individual plates. Garnish with a little chopped coriander and serve immediately.

Tasty Tip
Cooking the rice before grinding gives it a nutty, toasted flavour. Take care to only cook it until lightly browned and not at all blackened, as this would spoil the flavour. Chinese leaves make great serving containers for finger food.

Recipes: Vegetables

PACKED WITH
MONEY
SAVING
IDEAS
& TIPS

Thai Curry with Tofu

Ingredients (Serves 4)

750 ml/1¼ pts/3¼ cups coconut milk
700 g/1½ lb firm tofu, drained and cut into
  small cubes
salt and freshly ground black pepper
4 garlic cloves, peeled and chopped
1 large onion, peeled and cut into wedges
1 tsp crushed dried chillies
grated rind of 1 lemon
2.5-cm/1-in piece fresh root ginger, peeled
  and grated
1 tbsp ground coriander
1 tsp ground cumin
1 tsp turmeric
2 tbsp light soy sauce
1 tsp cornflour/cornstarch
Thai fragrant rice, to serve

TO GARNISH:
2 red chillies, deseeded and cut into rings
1 tbsp coriander/cilantro, freshly chopped
lemon wedges

Pour 600 ml/1 pt/2½ cups of the coconut milk into a saucepan and bring to the boil. Add the tofu, season to taste with salt and pepper and simmer gently for 10 minutes. Using a slotted spoon, remove the tofu and place on a plate. Reserve the coconut milk.

Place the garlic, onion, dried chillies, lemon rind, ginger, spices and soy sauce in a blender or food processor and blend until a smooth paste is formed. Pour the remaining 150 ml/ ¼ pt/²⁄₃ cup coconut milk into a clean saucepan and whisk in the spicy paste. Cook, stirring continuously, for 15 minutes, or until the curry sauce is very thick. Gradually whisk the reserved coconut milk into the curry and heat to simmering point. Add the cooked tofu and cook for 5–10 minutes. Blend the cornflour with 1 tablespoon of cold water and stir into the curry. Cook until thickened. Turn into a warmed serving dish and garnish with chilli, coriander and lemon wedges. Serve immediately with Thai fragrant rice.

Spicy Cucumber Stir-fry

Ingredients (Serves 4)

25 g/1 oz/3 tbsp black soya beans, soaked
  in cold water overnight
1½ cucumbers
2 tsp salt
1 tbsp groundnut/peanut oil
½ tsp mild chilli powder
4 garlic cloves, peeled and crushed
5 tbsp chicken stock
1 tsp sesame oil
1 tbsp freshly chopped parsley, to garnish

Rinse the soaked beans thoroughly, then drain. Place in a saucepan, cover with cold water and bring to the boil, skimming off any scum that rises to the surface. Boil for 10 minutes, then reduce the heat and simmer for 1–1½ hours. Drain and reserve.

Peel the cucumbers, slice lengthways and remove the seeds. Cut into 2.5-cm/1-in slices and place in a colander over a bowl. Sprinkle the salt over the cucumber and leave for 30 minutes. Rinse thoroughly in cold water, drain and pat dry with absorbent kitchen paper.

Heat a wok or large frying pan, add the oil and, when hot, add the chilli powder, garlic and black beans and stir-fry for 30 seconds. Add the cucumber and stir-fry for 20 seconds.

Pour the stock into the wok and cook for 3–4 minutes, or until the cucumber is very tender. The liquid will have evaporated at this stage. Remove from the heat and stir in the sesame oil. Turn into a warmed serving dish, garnish with chopped parsley and serve immediately.

Food Fact
Soya beans are the only pulse that contains all 8 essential amino acids, so they are an excellent source of protein. They are extremely dense and need to be soaked for at least 5 hours before cooking.

Thai-style Cauliflower and Potato Curry

Ingredients (Serves 4)

450 g/1 lb new potatoes, peeled and halved
    or quartered
350 g/12 oz/3 cups cauliflower florets
3 garlic cloves, peeled and crushed
1 onion, peeled and finely chopped
40 g/1½ oz/⅓ cup ground almonds
1 tsp ground coriander
½ tsp ground cumin
½ tsp turmeric
3 tbsp groundnut/peanut oil
salt and freshly ground black pepper
50 g/2 oz/¼ cup creamed coconut, broken
    into small pieces
200 ml/7 fl oz/¾ cup vegetable stock
1 tbsp mango chutney
sprigs of fresh coriander/cilantro, to garnish
freshly cooked long-grain rice, to serve

Bring a saucepan of lightly salted water to the boil, add the potatoes and cook for 15 minutes, or until just tender. Drain and leave to cool. Boil the cauliflower for 2 minutes, then drain and refresh under cold running water. Drain again and reserve.

Meanwhile, blend the garlic, onion, ground almonds and spices with 2 tablespoons of the oil and salt and pepper to taste in a food processor until a smooth paste is formed. Heat a wok, add the remaining oil and, when hot, add the spice paste and cook for 3–4 minutes, stirring continuously.

Dissolve the creamed coconut in 6 tablespoons of boiling water and add to the wok. Pour in the stock, cook for 2–3 minutes, then stir in the cooked potatoes and cauliflower.

Stir in the mango chutney and heat through for 3–4 minutes, or until piping hot. Tip into a warmed serving dish, garnish with sprigs of fresh coriander and serve immediately with freshly cooked rice.

Helpful Hint

Mildly flavoured vegetables absorb the taste and colour of the spices in this dish. Take care not to overcook the cauliflower; it should be only just tender for this dish. Broccoli florets would make a good alternative.

Black Bean Chilli with Avocado Salsa

Ingredients (Serves 4)

250 g/9 oz/1½ cups black beans and
    black-eye beans, soaked overnight
2 tbsp olive oil
1 large onion, peeled and finely chopped
1 red pepper/bell pepper, deseeded and diced
2 garlic cloves, peeled and finely chopped
1 red chilli, deseeded and finely chopped
2 tsp chilli powder
1 tsp ground cumin
2 tsp ground coriander
400 g/14 oz can chopped tomatoes
450 ml/¾ pt/2 cups vegetable stock
1 small ripe avocado, diced
½ small red onion, peeled and finely chopped
2 tbsp freshly chopped coriander/cilantro
juice of 1 lime
1 small tomato, peeled, deseeded and diced
salt and freshly ground black pepper
25 g/1 oz/1 square dark chocolate

TO GARNISH:
half-fat crème fraîche
lime slices
sprigs of coriander

Drain the beans and place in a large saucepan with at least twice their volume of fresh water. Bring slowly to the boil, skimming off any froth that rises to the surface. Boil rapidly for 10 minutes, then reduce the heat and simmer for 45 minutes, adding more water, if necessary. Drain and reserve.

Heat the oil in a large saucepan and add the onion and pepper. Cook for 3–4 minutes until softened. Add the garlic and chilli. Cook for 5 minutes, or until the garlic and chilli have softened. Add the chilli powder, cumin and coriander and cook for 30 seconds. Add the beans along with the tomatoes and stock. Bring to the boil and simmer, uncovered, for 40–45 minutes until the beans and vegetables are tender and the sauce has reduced.

Mix the avocado, onion, fresh coriander, lime juice and tomato. Season with salt and pepper. Remove the chilli from the heat. Break the chocolate into pieces. Sprinkle over the chilli. Leave for 2 minutes. Stir well. Garnish with crème fraîche, lime and coriander. Serve with the avocado salsa.

Chunky Vegetable and Fennel Goulash with Dumplings

Ingredients (Serves 4)

2 fennel bulbs, weighing about 450 g/1 lb
2 tbsp sunflower oil
1 large onion, peeled and sliced
1¹/₂ tbsp paprika
1 tbsp plain/all-purpose flour
300 ml/¹/₂ pt/1¹/₄ cups vegetable stock
400 g/14 oz can chopped tomatoes
450 g/1 lb potatoes, peeled and cut into
    2.5-cm/1-in chunks
125 g/4 oz small button mushrooms
salt and freshly ground black pepper

FOR THE DUMPLINGS:
1 tbsp sunflower oil
1 small onion, peeled and finely chopped
1 medium/large egg
3 tbsp milk
3 tbsp freshly chopped parsley
125 g/4 oz fresh white breadcrumbs

☑ Cut the fennel bulbs in half widthways. Thickly slice the stalks and cut the bulbs into 8 wedges. Heat the oil in a large saucepan or flameproof casserole. Add the onion and fennel and cook gently for 10 minutes until soft. Stir in the paprika and flour.

☑ Remove from the heat and gradually stir in the stock. Add the chopped tomatoes, potatoes and mushrooms. Season to taste with salt and pepper. Bring to the boil, reduce the heat and simmer for 20 minutes.

☑ Meanwhile, make the dumplings. Heat the oil in a frying pan and gently cook the onion for 10 minutes until soft. Leave to cool for a few minutes.

breadcrumb mixture into 12 round dumplings, each about the size of a walnut.

☑ Arrange the dumplings on top of the goulash. Cover and cook for a further 15 minutes, until the dumplings are cooked and the vegetables are tender. Serve immediately.

☑ In a bowl, beat the egg and milk together, then add the onion, parsley and breadcrumbs and season to taste. With damp hands, form the

Tasty Tip
Sour cream or crème fraîche is delicious spooned on top of the goulash.

Pumpkin and Chickpea Curry

Ingredients (Serves 4)

1 tbsp vegetable oil
1 small onion, peeled and sliced
2 garlic cloves, peeled and finely chopped
2.5-cm/1-in piece root ginger, peeled and grated
1 tsp ground coriander
$^{1}/_{2}$ tsp ground cumin
$^{1}/_{2}$ tsp ground turmeric
$^{1}/_{4}$ tsp ground cinnamon
2 tomatoes, chopped
2 red bird's eye chillies, deseeded and finely chopped
450 g/1 lb pumpkin or butternut squash flesh, cubed
1 tbsp hot curry paste
300 ml/$^{1}/_{2}$ pt/1$^{1}/_{4}$ cups vegetable stock
1 large firm banana
400 g/14 oz can chickpeas, drained and rinsed
salt and freshly ground black pepper
1 tbsp freshly chopped coriander/cilantro sprigs,
   to garnish
rice or naan bread, to serve

Heat 1 tablespoon of the oil in a saucepan and add the onion. Fry gently for 5 minutes until softened.

Add the garlic, ginger and spices and fry for a further minute. Add the chopped tomatoes and chillies and cook for another minute.

Add the pumpkin and curry paste and fry gently for 3–4 minutes before adding the stock.

Stir well, bring to the boil and simmer for 20 minutes until the pumpkin is tender.

Thickly slice the banana and add to the pumpkin along with the chickpeas. Simmer for a further 5 minutes.

Season to taste with salt and pepper and add the chopped coriander. Serve immediately, garnished with coriander sprigs and some rice or naan bread.

Helpful Hint

Curry pastes come in mild, medium and hot varieties. Although hot curry paste is recommended in this recipe, use whichever one you prefer.

Calypso Rice with Curried Bananas

Ingredients (Serves 4)

2 tbsp sunflower oil
1 medium onion, peeled and finely chopped
1 garlic clove, peeled and crushed
1 red chilli, deseeded and finely chopped
1 red pepper/bell pepper, deseeded and chopped
225 g/8 oz/1⅓ cups basmati rice
juice of 1 lime
350 ml/12 fl oz/1½ cups vegetable stock
200 g/7 oz can black-eye beans/peas, drained
    and rinsed
2 tbsp freshly chopped parsley
salt and freshly ground black pepper
sprigs of coriander/cilantro, to garnish

FOR THE CURRIED BANANAS:
4 green bananas
2 tbsp sunflower oil
2 tsp mild curry paste
200 ml/7 fl oz/¾ cup coconut milk

Heat the oil in a large frying pan and gently cook the onion for 10 minutes until soft. Add the garlic, chilli and red pepper and cook for 2–3 minutes.

Rinse the rice under cold running water, then add to the pan and stir. Pour in the lime juice and stock, bring to the boil, cover and simmer for 12–15 minutes, or until the rice is tender and the stock is absorbed. Stir in the black-eye beans and chopped parsley and season to taste with salt and pepper. Leave to stand, covered, for 5 minutes before serving, to allow the beans to warm through.

While the rice is cooking, make the curried green bananas. Remove the skins from the bananas – they may need to be cut off with a sharp knife. Slice the flesh thickly. Heat the oil in a frying pan and cook the bananas, in 2 batches, for 2–3 minutes, or until lightly browned. Pour the coconut milk into the pan and stir in the curry paste. Simmer, uncovered, over a low heat for 8–10 minutes, or until the bananas are very soft and the coconut milk slightly reduced.

Spoon the rice on to warmed serving plates, garnish with coriander and serve immediately with the curried bananas.

Panzanella

Ingredients (Serves 4)

250 g/9 oz loaf day-old Italian-style bread,
  such as ciabatta
1 tbsp red wine vinegar
4 tbsp olive oil
1 tsp lemon juice
1 small garlic clove, peeled and finely chopped
1 red onion, peeled and finely sliced
1 cucumber, peeled if preferred
2 medium ripe tomatoes, deseeded
150 g/5 oz/³/₄ cup pitted black olives
about 20 basil leaves, coarsely torn or
  left whole if small
sea salt and freshly ground black pepper

Cut the bread into thick slices, leaving the crusts on. Add 1 teaspoon of red wine vinegar to a jug of iced water, put the slices of bread in a bowl and pour over the water. Make sure the bread is covered completely. Leave to soak for 3–4 minutes until just soft.

Remove the soaked bread from the water and squeeze it gently, first with your hands and then in a clean tea towel to remove any excess water. Put the bread on a plate, cover with clingfilm/plastic wrap and chill in the refrigerator for about 1 hour.

Meanwhile, whisk together the olive oil, the remaining red wine vinegar and lemon juice in a large serving bowl. Add the garlic and onion and stir to coat well.

Halve the cucumber and remove the seeds. Chop both the cucumber and tomatoes into 1-cm/¹/₂-in dice. Add to the garlic and onions with the olives. Tear the bread into bite-sized chunks and add to the bowl with the fresh basil leaves. Toss together to mix and serve immediately with a grinding of sea salt and black pepper.

Budget Tip
Panzanella is sometimes referred to as a 'leftover salad' – it is a great way to use leftover bread. Why not try varying the other ingredients to suit your leftovers?

Pasta Shells with Broccoli and Capers

Ingredients (Serves 4)

400 g/14 oz/3½ cups conchiglie (pasta shells)
450 g/1 lb broccoli florets, cut into small pieces
5 tbsp olive oil
1 large onion, peeled and finely chopped
4 tbsp capers in brine, rinsed and drained
½ tsp dried chilli flakes (optional)
75 g/3 oz/¾ cup freshly grated Parmesan cheese,
  plus extra to serve
25 g/1 oz/¼ cup pecorino cheese, grated
salt and freshly ground black pepper
2 tbsp freshly chopped flat-leaf parsley, to garnish

Bring a large pan of lightly salted water to a rolling boil. Add the conchiglie, return to the boil and cook for 2 minutes. Add the broccoli to the pan. Return to the boil and continue cooking for 8–10 minutes, or until the conchiglie are *al dente*.

Meanwhile, heat the olive oil in a large frying pan, add the onion and cook for 5 minutes, or until softened, stirring frequently. Stir in the capers and chilli flakes, if using, and cook for a further 2 minutes.

Drain the pasta and broccoli and add to the frying pan. Toss the ingredients to

mix thoroughly. Sprinkle over the cheeses, then stir until the cheeses have just melted. Season to taste with salt and pepper, then tip into a warmed serving dish. Garnish with chopped parsley and serve immediately with extra Parmesan cheese.

Helpful Hint

Chilli flakes are made from dried, crushed chillies and add a pungent hot spiciness to this dish. There are lots of other chilli products that you could use instead. For instance, substitute a tablespoonful of chilli oil for one of the tablespoons of olive oil or add a dash of Tabasco sauce at the end of cooking.

Pad Thai Noodles with Mushrooms

Ingredients (Serves 4)

125 g/4 oz/2 cups flat rice noodles or rice vermicelli
1 tbsp vegetable oil
2 garlic cloves, peeled and finely chopped
1 medium/large egg, lightly beaten
225 g/8 oz/2 cups mixed mushrooms, including
   shiitake, oyster, field, brown and wild mushrooms
2 tbsp lemon juice
1½ tbsp Thai fish sauce
½ tsp sugar
½ tsp cayenne pepper
2 spring onions/scallions, trimmed and cut into
   2.5-cm/1-in pieces
50 g/2 oz/¼ cup fresh bean sprouts

TO GARNISH:
chopped roasted peanuts
freshly chopped coriander/cilantro

Cook the noodles according to the packet instructions. Drain well and reserve.

Heat a wok or large frying pan. Add the oil and garlic. Fry until just golden. Add the egg and stir quickly to break it up.

Cook for a few seconds before adding the noodles and mushrooms. Scrape down the sides of the pan to ensure they mix with the egg and garlic.

Add the lemon juice, fish sauce, sugar, cayenne pepper, spring onions and half the bean sprouts, stirring quickly all the time.

Cook over a high heat for a further 2–3 minutes until everything is heated through.

Turn on to a serving plate. Top with the remaining bean sprouts. Garnish with the chopped peanuts and coriander and serve immediately.

Budget Tip
Since this Pad Thai does not contain the usual prawn/shrimp or chicken element, this cuts down on costs.

Coconut-baked Courgettes

Ingredients (Serves 4)

3 tbsp groundnut/peanut oil
1 onion, peeled and finely sliced
4 garlic cloves, peeled and crushed
½ tsp chilli powder
1 tsp ground coriander
6–8 tbsp desiccated/dried coconut
1 tbsp tomato puree/paste
700 g/1½ lb courgettes/zucchini, thinly sliced
freshly chopped parsley, to garnish

Preheat the oven to 180°C/350°F/Gas Mark 4, 10 minutes before cooking. Lightly oil a large, shallow ovenproof gratin dish. Heat a wok, add the oil and, when hot, add the onion and stir-fry for 2–3 minutes, or until softened. Add the garlic, chilli powder and coriander and stir-fry for 1–2 minutes.

Pour 300 ml/½ pt/1¼ cups cold water into the wok and bring to the boil. Add the coconut and tomato puree and simmer for 3–4 minutes; most of the water will evaporate at this stage. Spoon 4 tablespoons of the spice and coconut mixture into a small bowl and reserve.

Stir the courgettes into the remaining spice and coconut mixture, coating well. Spoon the courgettes into the oiled gratin dish and sprinkle the reserved spice and coconut mixture evenly over the top. Bake, uncovered, in the preheated oven for 15–20 minutes, or until golden. Garnish with chopped parsley and serve immediately.

Helpful Hint

Because coconut is high in fat, desiccated/dried coconut has a relatively short shelf-life. Unless you use it in large quantities, buy it in small packets, checking the sell-by date. Once opened, it should be used within two months. If there is no sell-by date, smell the contents; it is easy to detect rancid coconut.

Mixed Vegetables Stir-fry

Ingredients (Serves 4)

2 tbsp groundnut/peanut oil
4 garlic cloves, peeled and finely sliced
2.5-cm/1-in piece fresh root ginger, peeled
  and finely sliced
75 g/3 oz/³⁄₄ cup broccoli florets
50 g/2 oz/heaped ¹⁄₂ cup mangetout/
  snowpeas, trimmed
1 carrot, peeled and cut into matchsticks
1 green pepper/bell pepper, deseeded and
  cut into strips
1 red pepper/bell pepper, deseeded and
  cut into strips
1 tbsp soy sauce
1 tbsp hoisin sauce
1 tsp sugar
salt and freshly ground black pepper
4 spring onions/scallions, trimmed and
  shredded, to garnish

Heat a wok, add the oil and when hot, add the garlic and ginger slices and stir-fry for 1 minute.

Add the broccoli florets to the wok, stir-fry for 1 minute, then add the mangetout, carrots and the green and red peppers and stir-fry for a further 3–4 minutes, or until tender but still crisp.

Blend the soy sauce, hoisin sauce and sugar in a small bowl. Stir well, season to taste with salt and pepper and pour into the wok. Transfer the vegetables to a warmed serving dish. Garnish with shredded spring onions and serve immediately with a selection of other Thai dishes.

Helpful Hint

Vary the combination of vegetables – try asparagus spears cut into short lengths, sliced mushrooms, French/green beans, red onion wedges and cauliflower florets.

Spinach Dhal

Ingredients (Serves 4-6)

100 g/4 oz/1 heaped cup split red lentils
2 onions, peeled and chopped
225 g/8 oz/2 cups potato, peeled and cut
    into small chunks
1 green chilli, deseeded and chopped
150 ml/¼ pt/⅔ cup water
1 tsp turmeric
175 g/6 oz/5⅘ cups fresh spinach
2 tomatoes, chopped
2 tbsp vegetable oil
1 tsp mustard seeds
few curry leaves

Rinse the lentils and place in a saucepan with the onions, potato, chilli, water and turmeric. Bring to the boil, then reduce the heat, cover and simmer for 15 minutes, or until the lentils are tender and most of the liquid has been absorbed.

Chop the spinach and add to the pan with the tomatoes and cook for a further 5 minutes, or until the spinach has wilted.

Heat the oil in a frying pan, add the mustard seeds and fry for 1 minute, or until they pop. Add the curry leaves, stir well then stir into the dhal and serve.

Helpful Hint

It is important that spices are stored correctly, otherwise their flavour can be impaired. Unless you use a lot of spice, buy in small quantities and store in a cool dark place. If you have time, grind your own spice powders to give a greater and more flavourful aroma and taste.

Sweet Potato Curry

Ingredients (Serves 4-6)

2 tbsp vegetable oil
2 green chillies, deseeded and chopped
5-cm/2-in piece fresh root ginger,
    peeled and grated
$^1/_2$–1 tsp chilli powder
1 tsp turmeric
1 tsp ground cumin
1 tsp ground coriander
2 onions, peeled and cut into wedges
2–3 garlic cloves, peeled and crushed
450 g/1 lb/3$^1/_3$ cups sweet potatoes, peeled
    and cut into small chunks
1 large green pepper/bell pepper, deseeded
    and chopped
4 tomatoes, chopped
300 ml/$^1/_2$ pt/1$^1/_4$ cups coconut milk
225 g/8 oz/7$^1/_2$ cups fresh spinach leaves
few curry leaves

Heat the oil in a sauté pan or wok, add the chillies, ginger and spices and fry for 3 minutes, stirring frequently. Add the onions and garlic and continue to fry for a further 5 minutes, or until the onions have softened.

Add the sweet potatoes and stir until coated in the spices, then add the green pepper and chopped tomatoes.

Pour in the coconut milk. Bring to the boil, then reduce the heat, cover and simmer for 12–15 minutes, or until the vegetables are cooked. Stir in the spinach and heat for 3 minutes, or until wilted.
Add the curry leaves, stir and serve.

Helpful Hint
As curry leaves are not that easy to find, it is worth buying a good number, then wrapping them well in freezer wrap and freezing.

Vegetable and Coconut Stew

Ingredients (Serves 4-6)

2 tbsp vegetable oil or ghee
1 tsp cumin seeds
1 cinnamon stick, bruised
3 whole cloves
3 cardamom pods, bruised
$^1/_2$–1 tsp chilli powder
8 shallots, peeled and halved
2–3 garlic cloves, peeled and finely chopped
225 g/8 oz/2 cups potatoes, peeled and cut
    into chunks
$^1/_2$ butternut squash, about 350 g/12 oz in weight,
    peeled, deseeded and cut into chunks
225 g/8 oz/1$^3/_4$ cups carrots, peeled and chopped
200 ml/7 fl oz/$^3/_4$ cup water
300 ml/$^1/_2$ pt/1$^1/_4$ cups coconut milk
225 g/8 oz/1$^1/_2$ cups French/green beans, trimmed
    and chopped
400 g/14 oz can red kidney beans, drained
    and rinsed
4–6 spring onions/scallions, trimmed and
    finely chopped

Heat the oil or ghee in a large saucepan, add the seeds, cinnamon stick, cloves, cardamom pods and chilli powder and fry for 30 seconds, or until the seeds pop.

Add the shallots, garlic, potatoes, squash and carrots and stir until the vegetables are coated in the flavoured oil. Add the water, bring to the boil, then reduce the heat, cover and simmer for 15 minutes.

Pour in the coconut milk and add the chopped beans and kidney beans. Stir well, then cook for a further 10 minutes. Sprinkle with the chopped spring onions and serve.

Vegetable and Lentil Casserole

Ingredients (Serves 4)

225 g/8 oz/1¼ cups Puy lentils
1–2 tbsp olive oil
1 onion, peeled and chopped
2–3 garlic cloves, peeled and crushed
300 g/10 oz/2⅓ cups carrots, peeled and
  sliced into chunks
3 celery stalks, trimmed and sliced
350 g/12 oz/2½ cups butternut squash, peeled,
  seeds removed and diced
1 l/1¾ pts/1 qt vegetable stock
salt and freshly ground black pepper
few sprigs of fresh oregano, plus extra to garnish
1 large red pepper/bell pepper, deseeded and chopped
2 courgettes/zucchini, trimmed and sliced
150 ml/¼ pt/⅔ cup sour cream, to serve

☑ Preheat the oven to 160°C/325°F/Gas Mark 3. Pour the lentils out on to a plate and look through them for any small stones, then rinse the lentils and reserve.

☑ Heat the oil in a large ovenproof casserole (or a deep frying pan, if preferred), add the onion, garlic, carrots and celery and sauté for 5 minutes, stirring occasionally.

☑ Add the squash and lentils. Pour in the stock and season to taste with salt and pepper. Add the oregano sprigs and bring to the boil.

☑ If a frying pan has been used, transfer everything to a casserole. Cover with a lid and cook in the oven for 25 minutes.

☑ Remove the casserole from the oven, add the red pepper and courgettes and stir. Return the casserole to the oven and cook for a further 20 minutes, or until all the vegetables are tender. Adjust the seasoning, garnish with sprigs of oregano and serve with sour cream on the side.

Tasty Tip
Other vegetables can be added to the casserole, such as sweet potatoes, aubergines/eggplants, turnips or parsnips.

Three Bean Tagine

Ingredients (Serves 4)

few saffron strands
2–3 tbsp olive oil
1 small aubergine/eggplant, trimmed and diced
1 onion, peeled and chopped
350 g/12 oz/2²/₃ cups sweet potatoes, peeled
   and diced
225 g/8 oz/1³/₄ cups carrots, peeled and chopped
1 cinnamon stick, bruised
1¹/₂ tsp ground cumin
salt and freshly ground black pepper
600 ml/1 pt/2¹/₂ cups vegetable stock
2 sprigs of fresh mint
200 g/7 oz can red kidney beans, drained
300 g/10 oz can haricot beans, drained
300 g/10 oz can flageolet beans, drained
125 g/4 oz/³/₄ cup ready-to-eat dried
   apricots, chopped
1 tbsp freshly chopped mint, to garnish

Place a small amount of warm water into a small bowl and sprinkle with saffron strands. Leave to infuse for at least 10 minutes.

Heat the oil in a large, heavy-based saucepan, add the aubergine and onion and sauté for 5 minutes before adding the sweet potato, carrots, cinnamon stick and ground cumin. Cook, stirring, until the vegetables are lightly coated in the cumin. Add the saffron with the soaking liquid and season to taste with salt and pepper. Pour in the stock and add the mint sprigs.

Rinse the beans, add to the pan and bring to the boil. Reduce the heat, cover with a lid and simmer for 20 minutes. Add the apricots and cook, stirring occasionally, for a further 10 minutes, or until the vegetables are tender. Adjust the seasoning to taste, then serve sprinkled with chopped mint.

Recipes: Deserts & Sweet Treats

PACKED WITH
• MONEY •
SAVING
IDEAS & TIPS

Lemon Surprise

Ingredients (Serves 4)

75 g/3 oz/¹/₂ stick reduced-fat butter or margarine
175 g/6 oz/⁷/₈ cup caster/superfine sugar
3 medium/large eggs, separated
75 g/3 oz/³/₄ cup self-raising flour
450 ml/³/₄ pt/2 cups semi-skimmed/reduced-fat milk
juice of 2 lemons
juice of 1 orange
2 tsp icing/confectioner's sugar
lemon twists, to decorate
sliced strawberries, to serve

Preheat the oven to 190°C/375°F/
Gas Mark 5. Lightly oil a deep
ovenproof dish.

Beat together the margarine and
sugar until pale and fluffy.

Add the egg yolks, one at a time, with
1 tablespoon of the flour and beat
well after each addition. Once added,
stir in the remaining flour.

Stir in the milk, 4 tablespoons of
the lemon juice and 3 tablespoons
of the orange juice.

Whisk the egg whites until stiff and
fold into the pudding mixture with a
metal spoon or rubber spatula until well
combined. Pour into the prepared dish.

Stand the dish in a roasting tin and
pour in just enough boiling water to
come halfway up the sides of the dish.

Bake in the preheated oven for
45 minutes, until well risen and
spongy to the touch.

Remove the pudding from the oven
and sprinkle with the icing sugar.
Decorate with the lemon twists and
serve immediately with strawberries.

Food Fact
This recipe uses a bain-marie (when
the dish is placed in a tin as in step 6),
which enables the pudding to cook
more slowly. This is necessary as half-fat
margarine does not respond well if
baked at high temperatures.

Coffee and Peach Creams

Ingredients (Serves 4)

4 peaches
50 g/2 oz/¼ cup caster/superfine sugar
2 tbsp coffee essence
200 g/7 oz carton low-fat Greek/plain yoghurt
300 g/11 oz carton low-fat ready-made
   custard (sauce)

TO DECORATE:
peach slices
sprigs of mint
low-fat crème fraîche

 Cut the peaches in half and remove the stones. Place the peaches in a large bowl, cover with boiling water and leave for 2–3 minutes.

 Drain the peaches, then carefully remove the skins. Using a sharp knife, halve the peaches.

Place the caster sugar in a saucepan and add 50 ml/2 fl oz/ ¼ cup water.

Bring the sugar mixture to the boil, stirring occasionally, until the sugar has dissolved. Boil rapidly for about 2 minutes.

 Add the peaches and coffee essence to the pan. Remove from the heat and allow the peach mixture to cool.

Meanwhile, mix together the yoghurt and custard until well combined.

Divide the peaches between four glass dishes.

Spoon over the custard mixture, then top with remaining peach mixture.

Chill for 30 minutes and then serve, decorated with peach slices, mint sprigs and a little crème fraîche.

Poached Pears

Ingredients (Serves 4)

2 small cinnamon sticks
125 g/4 oz/²⁄₃ cup caster/superfine sugar
300 ml/¹⁄₂ pt/1¹⁄₄ cups red wine
150 ml/¹⁄₄ pt/²⁄₃ cup water
thinly pared rind and juice of 1 small orange
4 firm pears
orange slices, to decorate
frozen vanilla yoghurt or low-fat ice cream, to serve

Place the cinnamon sticks on the work surface and, with a rolling pin, slowly roll down the side of the cinnamon stick to bruise. Place in a large, heavy-based saucepan.

Add the sugar, wine, water, pared orange rind and juice to the pan and bring slowly to the boil, stirring occasionally, until sugar is dissolved.

Meanwhile, peel the pears, leaving the stalks on.

Cut out the cores from the bottom of the pears and level them so that they stand upright.

Stand the pears in the syrup, cover the pan and simmer for 20 minutes or until tender.

Remove the pan from the heat and leave the pears to cool in the syrup, turning occasionally.

Arrange the pears on serving plates and spoon over the syrup. Decorate with the orange slices and serve with the yoghurt or low-fat ice cream and any remaining juices.

Tasty Tip
Poached pears are delicious served with a little crème fraîche and sprinkled with toasted almonds. To toast almonds, simply warm the grill/broiler and place whole, blanched almonds or flaked almonds on to a piece of kitchen foil. Place under the grill and toast lightly on both sides for 1–2 minutes until golden. Remove and cool, chop if liked.

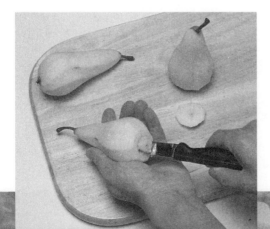

Chewy Choc and Nut Cookies

Ingredients (Makes 18)

15 g/½ oz/1 tbsp butter
4 medium/large egg whites
350 g/12 oz/3½ cups icing/confectioner's sugar
75 g/3 oz/¾ cup cocoa powder
2 tbsp plain/all-purpose flour
1 tsp instant coffee powder
125 g/4 oz/1 cup walnuts, finely chopped

Preheat the oven to 180°C/350°F/Gas Mark 4, 10 minutes before baking. Lightly butter several baking sheets with and line with a sheet of nonstick baking parchment. Place the egg whites in a large grease-free bowl and whisk with an electric mixer until the egg whites are very frothy.

Add the sugar, with the cocoa powder, the flour and coffee powder and whisk again until the ingredients are blended thoroughly. Add 1 tablespoon of water and continue to whisk on the highest speed until the mixture is very thick. Fold in the chopped walnuts.

Place tablespoons of the mixture on to the prepared baking sheets, leaving plenty of space between them as they expand greatly during cooking.

Bake in the preheated oven for 12–15 minutes, or until the tops are firm, golden and quite cracked. Leave to cool for 30 seconds, then, using a spatula, transfer to a wire rack and leave to cool. Store in an airtight tin.

Tasty Tip
Although the walnuts in these biscuits are excellent, hazelnuts or mixed nuts would also go very well with both the chocolate and the coffee flavours.

Marbled Chocolate Traybake

Ingredients (Makes 18 Squares)

175 g/6 oz/1½ sticks butter
175 g/6 oz/⅞ cup caster/superfine sugar
1 tsp vanilla essence
3 medium/large eggs, lightly beaten
200 g/7 oz/1½ cups self-raising flour
½ tsp baking powder
1 tbsp milk
1½ tbsp cocoa powder

FOR THE CHOCOLATE ICING/FROSTING:
75 g/3 oz/3 squares plain dark/bittersweet chocolate,
   broken into pieces
75 g/3 oz/3 squares white chocolate, broken
   into pieces

Preheat the oven to 180°C/350°F/Gas Mark 4, 10 minutes before baking. Oil and line a 28 x 18 x 2.5 cm/11 x 7 x 1 in cake tin/pan with nonstick baking parchment. Cream the butter, sugar and vanilla essence until light and fluffy. Gradually add the eggs, beating well after each addition. Sift in the flour and baking powder and fold in with the milk.

Spoon half the mixture into the prepared tin, spacing the spoonfuls apart and leaving gaps in between. Blend the cocoa powder to a smooth paste with 2 tablespoons of warm water. Stir this into the remaining cake mixture. Drop small spoonfuls between the vanilla cake mixture to fill in all the gaps. Use a knife to swirl the mixtures together a little.

Bake on the centre shelf of the preheated oven for 35 minutes, or until well risen and firm to the touch. Leave in the tin for 5 minutes to cool, then turn out on to a wire rack and leave to cool. Remove the parchment.

For the icing, place the plain and white chocolate in separate heatproof bowls and melt each over a saucepan of almost boiling water. Spoon into separate nonstick baking parchment piping bags, snip off the tips and drizzle over the top. Leave to set before cutting into squares.

Fruit and Nut Flapjacks

Ingredients (Makes 12)

75 g/3 oz/²/₃ stick butter or margarine
125 g/4 oz/³/₄ cup soft light brown sugar
3 tbsp golden/corn syrup
50 g/2 oz/¹/₂ cup raisins
50 g/2 oz/¹/₂ cup walnuts, roughly chopped
175 g/6 oz/1 scant cup rolled oats/oatmeal
50 g/2 oz/5 tbsp icing/confectioner's sugar
1–1¹/₂ tbsp lemon juice

Preheat the oven to 180°C/350°F/Gas Mark 4, 10 minutes before baking. Lightly oil a 23-cm/9-in square cake tin/pan.

Melt the butter or margarine with the sugar and syrup in a small saucepan over a low heat. Remove from the heat.

Stir the raisins, walnuts and oats into the syrup mixture and mix together well.

Spoon evenly into the prepared tin and press down well. Transfer to the preheated oven and bake for 20–25 minutes.

Remove from the oven and leave to cool in the tin. Cut into bars while still warm.

Sift the icing sugar into a small bowl, then gradually beat in the lemon juice a little at a time to form a thin icing.

Place into a piping bag fitted with a writing nozzle, then pipe thin lines over the flapjacks. Allow to cool and serve.

Tasty Tip
These flapjacks/oat bars are packed with energy, but why not increase the nutritional value by adding a few tablespoons of seeds, such as sesame, sunflower and pumpkin seeds, then adding some chopped up ready-to-eat fruit such as apricot, pineapple or mango? You can also add chocolate cooking chips, chopped glacé fruits as well as currants and sultanas.

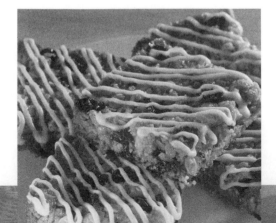

Crunchy Rhubarb Crumble

Ingredients (Serves 6)

125 g/4 oz/1 cup plain/all-purpose flour
50 g/2 oz/¼ cup softened butter
50 g/2 oz/⅔ cup rolled oats/oatmeal
50 g/2 oz/4 tbsp Demerara/brown sugar
1 tbsp sesame seeds
½ tsp ground cinnamon
450 g/1 lb fresh rhubarb
50 g/2 oz/4 tbsp caster/superfine sugar
custard (sauce) or cream, to serve

Preheat the oven to 180°C/350°F/Gas Mark 4. Place the flour in a large bowl and cut the butter into cubes. Add to the flour and rub in with the fingertips until the mixture looks like fine breadcrumbs, or blend for a few seconds in a food processor.

Stir in the rolled oats, demerara sugar, sesame seeds and cinnamon. Mix well and reserve.

Prepare the rhubarb by removing the thick ends of the stalks and cutting them diagonally into 2.5-cm/1-in chunks. Wash thoroughly and pat dry with a clean tea towel. Place the rhubarb in a 1.1-l/2-pt/1-qt pie dish.

Sprinkle the caster sugar over the rhubarb and top with the reserved crumble mixture. Level the top of the crumble so that all the fruit is well covered and press down firmly. If liked, sprinkle the top with a little extra caster sugar.

Place on a baking sheet and bake in the preheated oven for 40–50 minutes, or until the fruit is soft and the topping is golden brown. Sprinkle the pudding with some more caster sugar and serve hot with custard or cream.

Cherry Batter Pudding

Ingredients (Serves 4)

450 g/1 lb fresh cherries (or 425 g/16 oz can
   pitted cherries)
50 g/2 oz/⅓ cup plain/all-purpose flour
pinch of salt
3 tbsp caster/superfine sugar
2 medium/large eggs
300 ml/½ pt/1¼ cups milk
40 g/1½ oz/3 tbsp butter
1 tbsp rum
extra caster/superfine sugar, to dredge
fresh cream, to serve

 Preheat the oven to 220°C/425°F/Gas Mark 7. Lightly oil a 900-ml/1½-pt/ 1-qt shallow baking dish.

 Rinse the cherries, drain well and remove the stones (using a cherry

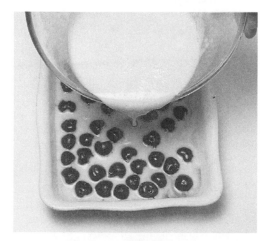

stoner, if possible). If using canned cherries, drain well, discard the juice and place in the prepared dish.

 Sift the flour and salt into a large bowl. Stir in 2 tablespoons of the caster sugar and make a well in the centre. Beat the eggs, then pour into the well of the dry ingredients.

 Warm the milk and slowly pour into the well, beating throughout and gradually drawing in the flour from the sides of the bowl. Continue until a smooth batter has formed.

 Melt the butter in a small saucepan over a low heat, then stir into the batter with the rum. Reserve for 15 minutes, then beat again until smooth and easy to pour.

 Pour into the prepared baking dish and bake in the preheated oven for 30–35 minutes, or until golden brown and set.

 Remove the pudding from the oven, sprinkle with the remaining sugar and serve hot with plenty of fresh cream.

Index